ADVENTURES IN THE

WILDERNESS

ADVENTURES IN

FIRST EDITION

THE WILDERNESS

BY THE EDITORS OF
AMERICAN HERITAGE
The Magazine of History

AUTHOR
RUTHERFORD PLATT

CONSULTANT
HORACE M. ALBRIGHT
Former Director, National Park Service

PUBLISHED BY
AMERICAN HERITAGE
PUBLISHING CO., INC.,
New York

BOOK TRADE DISTRIBUTION BY
MEREDITH PRESS

INSTITUTIONAL DISTRIBUTION BY
HARPER & ROW

In 1858 Ralph Waldo Emerson and fourteen friends were painted at their wilderness retreat in the Adirondack Mountains. The men gathered here regularly to study nature.

6

Foreword

The most precious possession of any people is its land. Certainly, Americans have been well served by the continent on which they live; nowhere else on earth is there a land so favored. Today we tend to take this heritage for granted, but to the men from Europe who first saw the American wilderness, its seemingly endless forests, prairies, deserts, and mountains posed a fearsome challenge. How they met that challenge is told in this book.

This majestic wilderness had evolved over the course of millions upon millions of years. Animals and plants thrived there in an abundance that staggered the early explorers and settlers; over each hill they found new wonders. But for all its abundance and beauty, it was often an unforgiving, alien land, in effect an enemy to be conquered. In the conquering, they frequently upset the delicate balance of nature, then moved on without a backward glance.

Along with these hard-handed men came artists who stopped to record the wonders of the wilderness. Their sketches and paintings give a glimpse of creatures that once roamed the land by the millions but today exist only in limited numbers, or do not exist at all. Through their eyes can be seen the wild beauty of America before it was tamed—and too often marred—by the hand of man.

There also came the conservationists trying to save what wilderness was left, and to some extent they have been successful. Our two newest states, Alaska and Hawaii, have contributed a wilderness heritage that enriches our natural treasury. Yet self-appointed prophets of progress, marching in step behind their bulldozers, are even now intent on raiding this treasury.

The American wilderness has put its stamp on the American character. The strength, courage, and endurance needed to explore the land and to reap its bounty have stood us in good stead for more than four and a half centuries. Now these same traits are needed to preserve what remains.

The Editors

COVER: *Frontier scouts atop a high
bluff scan the prairie wilderness for
Indian war parties in this 1851
painting by William T. Ranney.*
M. KNOEDLER & COMPANY, NEW YORK

FRONT ENDSHEET: *John White's map
shows the geography of the eastern
coast from Virginia to Florida as
it was known to Europe about 1600.*
BRITISH MUSEUM

BACK ENDSHEET: *Swiss-born Karl
Bodmer pictured a hunter stalking
dangerous grizzly bears along the
upper Missouri River in the 1830's.*
YALE UNIVERSITY LIBRARY

This first drawing of the American bison, or buffalo, is dated 1554.

Contents

ILLUSTRATED WITH PAINTINGS, PRINTS, DRAWINGS,
AND MAPS, MANY OF THE PERIOD

1

Origins of the Wilderness

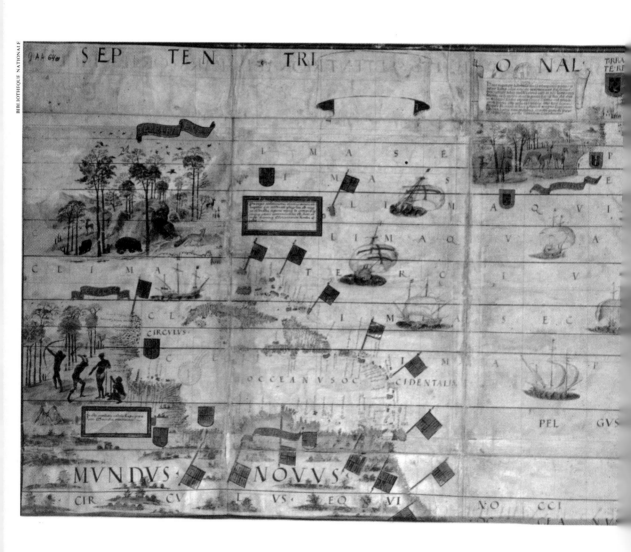

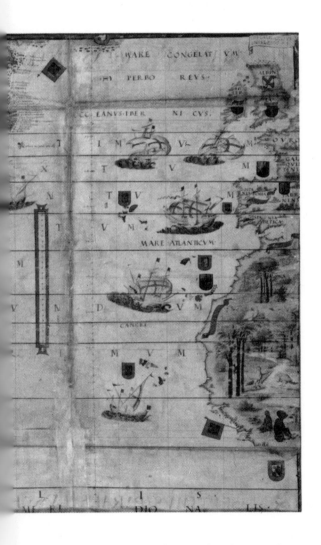

Christopher Columbus never set foot on the North American mainland. His first sight of the New World was a sandy island in the Bahamas. He did not know that a little to the northwest lay eight million square miles of wilderness of incredible variety—deep forests, vast swamps, flowering deserts, oceans of prairie grass, snow-topped volcanoes, lakes like inland seas, immense rivers and waterfalls, and the deepest and most awesome canyon in the world.

Long before Columbus, other Europeans had glimpsed the edges of this great wilderness. The first were the Vikings of northern Europe. These sea-wanderers followed a water path westward to lands jutting out into the dim Atlantic; and although they kept no records, stories of strange shores were handed down from seafaring father to seafaring son.

The earliest of the Viking tales is that of Bjarni, an adventurer who was thrown off course by storms and fog

Europeans were furnished with unusual views of life in the New World by this decorative map done about 1519. The flags mark Spain's footholds in the Caribbean area, but America (upper left) is only imagined.

between Iceland and Greenland about the year 985. He first sighted a land "without mountains, well timbered"; turning northwest, he saw land again, "a flat country covered with timber." Three days later he made a third sighting, this time "high and mountainous with ice upon it." Bjarni did not put ashore, for the land appeared to him to be "good for nothing."

Bjarni's landfalls were probably southern Labrador, then northern Labrador, and finally, before turning back toward Greenland, the snow-covered mountains of Baffin Island. More important, he was the first European to glimpse North America.

At about this time Norsemen settled in Greenland. For a century their light ships, built like war canoes with single square sails, slipped through the gloomy waters between Greenland and America, reaching as far south as Cape Cod. Reports of their visits to the American wilderness were told as personal adventures, until they became the sagas of the Norsemen, part legend and part history.

The Norse name for this wilderness was Vinland or Vineland, after what impressed them most there—the wild grapes. Nothing like them grew in either Iceland or Greenland. But along the coast of New England they found grape stems six inches in diameter, running to the tops of trees and spreading a dense canopy over acres of woodland.

The Norsemen also admired the tall, straight spruces that fronted the sea along other parts of the coast. But aside from these few facts and their troubles with the Indians (whom they called *skraellings,* or "wretched people"), little is known of the wilderness as the Vikings first saw it. Later, the Greenland colonies, which were the threshold to America, mysteriously disappeared. Men who went to look for them after hundreds of years found only the stone foundations of houses and barns.

Meanwhile, European explorers were looking eastward rather than to the west. The lands of the east, the Orient or Indies, were in the mind of the Genoese navigator Christopher Columbus, who sailed from Spain in August, 1492, with a hope so daring that it sounded mad—the hope of reaching the east by sailing west. When he landed in the Bahamas, so confident was he that he had reached the Indies, he named the natives he found Indians.

Explorers who came after Columbus still had their hearts set on finding a way to the Indies. The first white man known to have seen the Middle Atlantic coast was a Florentine named Verrazano. In 1524 he looked across a sandspit—the Outer Banks of North Carolina—at Pamlico Sound, and identified it as the Pacific Ocean. He was overjoyed to discover that America at this point was no more than a mile wide.

Verrazano sailed northward, searching for a channel through the "mile-wide" continent. Soon he passed

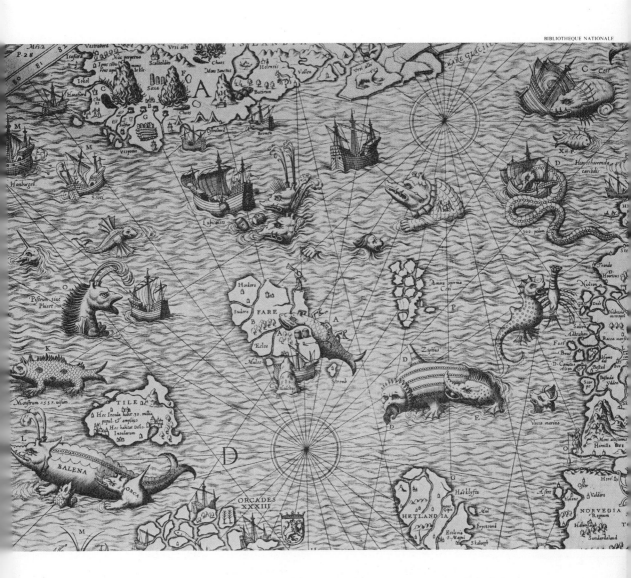

Tales of monsters lurking in the waters off the New World haunted European explorers in the 1500's, when this chart of the North Atlantic was drawn. The artist suggested throwing barrels overboard and blowing trumpets (as the men on the ship above the island at center are doing) to drive off sea serpents.

through the Narrows into what is now New York harbor, and traveled a short way up the Hudson River. But the steep cliffs of the Palisades did not seem to promise a route to Asia, and he headed back out to sea. Ten years later Jacques Cartier, a Frenchman also in search of a Northwest Passage to Asia, became the discoverer of the Gulf of St. Lawrence.

But these explorers only touched the American wilderness. No white man had yet penetrated it. Then, in the middle of the sixteenth century, three humble English seamen, David Ingram, Richard Browne, and Richard Twide, challenged this forbidding land.

In 1568 Ingram and his companions sailed into the Gulf of Mexico aboard the *Minion,* part of a small fleet commanded by the buccaneer and adventurer John Hawkins. After a disastrous battle with a Spanish squadron, the *Minion,* nearly swamped with survivors, drifted alone in the broad Gulf. Preferring to take their chances on land rather than starve on the voyage back to England, Ingram, Browne, Twide, and 111 others put ashore on the Mexican coast.

Twenty-three of the sailors struck out northward to avoid being captured by the Spanish; twenty of them disappeared forever. But Ingram, Browne, and Twide kept on toward the North Star. A year later, in October, 1569, a French sea captain sighted the three men on a bleak headland of Nova Scotia and rescued them. They

had walked through 3,000 miles of primeval wilderness.

After his return to England, David Ingram prepared the story of his wanderings for a commission from the court of Queen Elizabeth that was seeking information about the New World. Ingram tried to please the fine and important gentlemen who questioned him, and his story is a strange mixture of what he actually saw, what he thought his questioners wanted to hear, and wild sailor's yarns.

In this fabulous New World were bright wild flowers, pink flamingos, and buffalo with "eares like a bludde hownde"—plus penguins, white bears, leopards, and elephants in the green woods. He recalled the slow red streams of the south, the rivers "some foure . . . some eight . . . some tenne miles over" of what is now Maryland and Delaware, and the harsh granite coast of Maine. He particularly remembered "a kinde of Graine, the eare whereof is as big as the wrist"—corn on the cob.

Ingram's account is laced with things hoped for rather than seen—nuggets of gold as big as a man's fist, and native kings, wearing four-inch rubies, who were carried in chairs of gold and crystal. Nevertheless, he and his companions were the first white men to test the great American wilder-

Countless centuries before the appearance of land animals, swampy forests of fernlike trees and shrubs covered much of America. Charles Knight's painting of this plant domain is based on fossils 350 million years old.

Among the first animals fossilized in the rocks of this continent were the simple marine trilobites at top. More complex organisms, like the fern and the fish, thrived later, but they too left only fossils as mute evidence of their existence.

ness and live to tell about it, and they made what is still the longest trek ever recorded through the eastern part of North America.

By the seventeenth century, explorers, traders, and adventurers, lured by the prospect of wealth in gold or furs, or simply by the unknown, were penetrating the American wilderness all along the Atlantic seaboard. Following streams and the trails of Indians and animals, they wondered at its vast dimensions—the height of mountains, the extent of forests, the countless numbers of birds and animals. But there was yet another dimension to the wilderness of which they were unaware—the dimension of time.

The forests, rivers, and mountains seemed timeless, as though they had always been there. But the wilderness seen by those early explorers was instead a product of continuous and unending change. It had been altered in the six hundred years since Norsemen first saw it. As striking as these changes may have been, they were small compared to the stupendous, slow-moving changes which have occurred through the processes of geology and evolution.

The earth's crust, solid and permanent as it appears from the rocks that compose it, is actually neither solid nor permanent. The hot, molten core of the earth is in a state of constant upheaval, producing shifts and foldings and bucklings of the earth's outer layers. Such disturbances produced many mountain ranges—the Appalachians and the Rockies, for instance.

Other mountains were created by more sudden means—the underground explosions that produce volcanoes and earthquakes. Mt. Rainier in Washington and the mountains of Hawaii are of this type. Upon all these mountains, and upon the earth's entire surface, the winds, the rains, the rivers, the cycle of freezing and thawing, are even now causing changes, slowly but unceasingly, year by year, hour by hour.

Along with these alterations in the earth's surface have gone alterations, no less remarkable, in the plants and animals living there. Many of these changes took place long before there were human beings to record them. Nevertheless, the earth itself contains a record, by means of fossil remains, of once-flourishing animals and plants unlike any living today.

These fossils are often found in unexpected places. For example, buried deep in mountainsides 1,000 feet above Palm Springs, California, are large beds of oyster shells. In New York State and in the Middle West, far from any ocean, there are deposits of limestone containing the remains of sea animals—sharks' teeth among them. Bones, teeth, and footprints of dinosaurs—huge extinct ancestors of the snakes, turtles, and alligators of today—have been found in great numbers east of Salt Lake City. Not long ago, a flash flood in the Catskill Mountains of New York uncovered the petrified stumps of strange fern trees, forty feet high and three feet in diameter, which grew there 300 million years ago.

From such records, and from observations of plants and animals now living, scientists have been able to put together a picture—though incomplete and in many places uncertain—of that process of change in living things called evolution. They do not know just how life began, but they do know that it began in the water. The oldest fossil remains, as dated by the methods of geology, are of aquatic forms of life. At some point in the slow processes of evolution, some of these living things acquired the ability to live on land.

It seems fairly certain that plants made the transition first. By the Carboniferous Age—the period when coal deposits were formed from the compressed remains of plants—the first land animals had made their appearance, some 280 million years ago. In coal beds in Pennsylvania there are fossil remains of cockroaches four inches long; dragonflies with thirty-inch wingspreads; and giant forerunners of our scorpions, spiders, and centipedes. These nightmarish creatures lived in hot swamps where club mosses and fernlike plants grew to the size of trees.

Some sort of upheaval, still not clearly understood, brought a gradual end to the warm, humid climate of the Carboniferous Age. Slowly, over millions of years, a new era took form, the Age of Reptiles. The North Amer-

Ranging in size from a few pounds to forty tons, the dinosaurs ruled the raw wilderness for 100 million years. The largest was the Brontosaurus (right); its bones have been unearthed in many western states. These huge monsters were harmless compared to the smaller, flesh-eating Dryptosaurus (above). Below, as winged reptiles swoop overhead, a prehistoric serpent attacks its prey in the ocean which covered part of the continent.

18

ican climate was still warm, but the landscape was less swampy, consisting instead of low, rolling hills and valleys. The first seed plants appeared, although as yet there were no true flowers, no bushes, no grass.

Temperatures were mild the year around, and tremendous cloudbursts sent down surging floods which gathered into countless lakes and ponds. Flashes of lightning revealed monsters with long necks and tails, swimming in the lakes and browsing among the weird trees that grew along these waterways. These were the dinosaurs, the Greek word for "terrible lizards." Some were the size of small dogs. Others were the biggest brutes that ever walked the earth.

These reptiles, great and small, were masters of the continent for perhaps 100 million years, much longer than any other kind of animal has ever dominated the land. But with yet another upheaval, the dinosaur empire collapsed. The middle of the North American continent sank; the Middle West became an inland sea, with its eastern shore near what is now Pittsburgh. At the same time, to the west, the rock of the earth's crust was lifted, and in some places it cracked and tilted to form the Rocky Mountains.

With these elemental events came an equally major change in the climate. Temperature and rainfall became more variable, as they are today. Into this environment, again by the process of evolutionary change lasting millions of years, came flowering plants and warm-blooded animals and birds. The descendants of the mighty dinosaurs evolved into the small snakes, lizards, turtles, and alligators of the American wilderness.

Curiously, a few plants of the kind on which the dinosaurs fed still exist. The cycads, palmlike trees with some features of ferns but with seed-bearing cones rather like those of a pine tree, are found in Florida and Hawaii. And the ginkgo, which has leaves like a maidenhair fern and which somehow survived as a wild plant in China, now thrives in this country where few other trees can live at all—in the polluted air and amidst the concrete pavements of our big cities.

By the end of the Age of Reptiles the flowering plants had become more conspicuous than the cycads and ginkgos. Soon the first birds and mammals appeared, although hardly recognizable as such. Both developed from reptilian ancestors which have long since become extinct. The first mammals were tiny creatures no bigger than mice, like opossums and shrews in their habits. In Europe and in Asia mammal types gradually evolved over millions of years into grazing animals, such as the buffalo and the horse, or into carnivores like the wildcat and the wolf.

While these familiar types were developing, there roamed over the North American continent a strange assortment of outlandish animals, known today only by their fossils. There were great woolly mammoths, wild pigs the

size of the hippopotamus, spotted leopard-like sabertooths, and tiny horses no bigger than dogs. Equally strange was an abundance of camels.

The key to the mystery of the migration of animals to the American wilderness is the so-called Bering land bridge. Alaska and Siberia are now separated by the shallow, fifty-six-mile-wide Bering Strait; here the continents of Asia and North America are part of the same land mass, joined by a low-lying isthmus that happens at present to be under water. During much of the time in ages past, however, it has been dry land. If the water level of the ocean were but two hundred feet lower, as it has been many times in the past, the uncovered isthmus would have a width of more than a thousand miles.

The forerunners of our bison and bighorn sheep, of our bears, deer, and elk, of our beavers and squirrels, arrived from Asia over the Bering land bridge. Other native American animals never made the trip at all. The prairie dog, for instance, has no counterpart in the Old World. Neither does the graceful pronghorn, which, though often called the antelope, had an evolution entirely separate from the true antelope of India and Africa.

The land bridge was not, of course, the only route by which the spread and change of living things took place. Birds had taken to the air before the Age of Reptiles ended. The ancestors of the great auk of the Labrador coast, for example, may have made their way

The world owes much of its knowledge of dinosaurs to the brilliant work of an American scientist named Edward Drinker Cope. Revealing a wry sense of humor (below) in his field sketches, Cope found and classified many fossil types during the late 1800's.

westward by island-hopping across the North Atlantic. Seals could swim; polar bears, which hunted and still hunt these flippered fur-bearers, might ride hundreds of miles on ice floes in times of an Arctic thaw. The hardy musk ox, equipped for subzero weather, could easily have wandered over the frozen polar seas from Asia to America.

Some 35,000 years ago, mountainous glaciers, compacted of ton upon ton of snow, rose just west of Hudson Bay and in Labrador. Their massive domes rose to a height of three miles, and the pressure of that great weight sent lobes of ice flowing as far southward as the sites of today's cities of New York and St. Louis. This was the last phase of the Ice Age. Underneath the glaciers the rocky crust of the continent sagged several hundred feet. At the same time, so much water had evaporated from the oceans, to be locked up in the glaciers, that as the ice advanced, the level of the sea continued to fall.

The Bering land bridge, exposed by the shrinking of the seas, was like the tundra of northern Canada today. There were thickets of blueberry and crowberry bushes, scattered spruce forests, plains bordered by stunted aspens and birch trees, and grassy meadows that provided hiding places for rabbits and quail. Glacier-covered mountains, far to the east, sparkled in the sun. Strangely enough, in northwestern Alaska there was no ice except on the mountains. The land bridge

AMERICAN MUSEUM OF NATURAL HISTORY

At the close of the Ice Age the slowly retreating glaciers (above) exposed startling changes in the face of America. Valleys, river beds, and rocky crags had been carved or thrust up by the enormous pressure of the ice. Remarkable forms of life also appeared on the continent as the glaciers departed. Woolly mammoths (right), shaggy predecessors of today's elephants, were among the animals that crossed from Asia to the New World on the Bering land bridge.

was clear although much of the rest of the continent lay under the ice. It was then that the first human migrants crossed the Bering land bridge into North America.

They were Mongol people living in the late Stone Age. They made spear-points from flint rock, and their clothes were the skins of bear and musk ox. This movement of people across the land bridge was no sudden rush; rather, it took place gradually. Family groups camped for years on the land bridge itself. They were hunters and fishermen; always ahead of them, to the east, were the tracks of animals—musk ox, moose, bear, beaver, rabbit—to draw them on and on into the American wilderness.

Gradually the weather grew warmer, the Ice Age faded, and the glaciers melted. The people moved eastward along the low Arctic seacoast of Alaska, and then turned south to follow the Mackenzie River valley. They prospered in the virgin wilderness. Their numbers increased. They learned how to make new tools and weapons out of the bones of animals and the wood of trees in the New World.

The families grew into tribes, and the tribes slowly spread across the mountains and deserts and plains and woodlands of North America. Moving still farther southward, they became the founders of the glittering civilizations of the Aztecs on the Mexican plateau, the Maya in Yucatán, the Inca in the mountains of Peru.

So the New World was populated and the stage set for the arrival of the vanguard of explorers from the Old World. The Indian lived at peace with the wilderness; the white man would not be content until he had conquered it.

Pictorial records of American wildlife had been kept by Indians for centuries before the coming of the white men. The mural of an antelope hunt (above) was discovered in an Arizona canyon first inhabited by Indians in the third century. The Plains Indian calendar at right, in which years are represented by tepees, was decorated with a buffalo by a Sioux warrior whose very existence depended on this animal.

2

The Coastal Fringe

The Europeans who discovered and explored the American wilderness found its wonders intact. Indian trails crossed much of it, but the tread of moccasined feet and the twang of bows did no harm to the vitality of the wilderness. The people were in balance with the animals, fish, and birds. The land created in the battles of the elements through the ages had emerged from volcanic fires, invading seas, and massive glaciers, with wealth enough to support both Indians and wildlife in natural prosperity.

A vast woodland, green and sun-flecked, stretched almost unbroken from the Atlantic coast to the Mississippi River. Between the Mississippi and the Rocky Mountains lay the grassy ocean of the prairies and the Great Plains. To the north, spreading well into what is now Canada and extending to the Pacific, were dark evergreen forests of spruce and fir. To the southwest lay a desert region, starkly colored from the minerals in the raw sand and rock. Honking squadrons of wild geese filled the night, and iridescent millions of passenger pigeons darkened the daytime sky.

In the desert Indians had built villages, called pueblos. On the open

Colonizer William Penn first saw his spectacular New World domain of Pennsylvania in October, 1682. Painted here in romantic fashion by Thomas Birch, Penn was moved by the autumn beauty of his landfall.

prairies they pursued coyotes, antelope, and great hump-backed bison, or buffalo. In the eastern woods they hunted deer and wild turkey, trapped beaver, fished in lakes and streams, and grew corn, pumpkins, potatoes, beans, and tobacco. Those in the northern spruce forest took the bear in his lair, trapped the muskrat, stalked the moose and caribou, and pursued the migrating salmon.

The coming of the white men upset this delicate natural balance. They cut over and burned the forests, dammed the streams, and drained the swamps. And they senselessly slaughtered animals and birds by the thousands. There is, for example, the brutal fate of the great auk.

In the early summer of 1534, the French explorer Jacques Cartier came in sight of waves breaking on a low, rocky island—known today as Funk Island—off the coast of Newfoundland. Sailors usually head away from dangerous breakers, but Cartier's famished crew shouted and clapped each other on the back at what they saw. Ambling over the rocks were what looked like a crowd of little men, white-fronted and black-backed as though they were in formal dress. These were the stately great auks, standing over two feet high. They could not fly, and they were clumsy on land, but in the ocean these creatures were as graceful as dolphins.

The great auks had been hatching their eggs on Funk Island and on nearby places like it for thousands of years, safely out of reach of such hungry mammals as raccoons, foxes, and weasels. They had never learned to run from anything. When Cartier's crew appeared, the auks simply stood quietly as the men clubbed them to death. Cartier wrote that within half an hour their landing boats were nearly swamped with carcasses.

After that, for three centuries, ships crossing the North Atlantic anchored at Funk Island to kill the great auks. In calm weather the crews even laid gangplanks between the rocks and the ships, and the gentle birds obligingly marched to their doom. The thick coats of fat which kept them warm in icy waters became oil for ships' lanterns; salted down, their flesh made the tastiest stew known aboard any ship. The end came in 1844, when the last pair of great auks alive in the world was killed on a rocky islet off the coast of Iceland.

Since that day the passenger pigeon, the heath hen, the Labrador duck, the Carolina parakeet, the Eskimo curlew, and the ivory-billed woodpecker have also vanished because of the harmful effect of the white man on the wilderness in which these creatures lived.

On the other hand, there are some creatures so prolific that, though taken in vast quantities for food, they have never been in danger of extinction. One of these is the cod, a fish living by countless millions in the cold waters off the coast of Newfoundland. In 1497, on a voyage of exploration for England, John and Sebastian Cabot

This John J. Audubon engraving of a pair of great auks was made in 1836; within eight years the handsome birds were extinct, ruthlessly slaughtered for food and feathers by crews of ships plying the North Atlantic.

reported that they could hardly push their ships through these waters because of the teeming cod. Soon the cod were to the fishermen of Europe what gold was to the Spanish conquerors of South America.

The cod which still flourishes and the great auk which became extinct both fed mainly on capelin, a six-inch fish just the right size for a mouthful. On a fair day the auks stood at the edge of the sea watching the color of the water. When they saw a dark patch, made by ripples above a school of capelin driven inshore by pursuing cod, the auks dove in to meet the oncoming feast.

The capelin feed on young herring, which are still smaller, while the food of those silvery little fish consists of tiny, barely visible shrimps. These minute shrimps keep alive in their turn by feeding mainly on diatoms—microscopic plants which in cold northern waters make up the plankton that is the pasture of the sea.

Diatoms seen under a microscope are wonderful things, lovely as jewels. What makes them all the more wonderful is that without the power they have of harnessing sunlight to manufacture their own food—a power which no animal has—life in the sea could not go on, any more than it could on land if there were no green plants.

For the great auks, for their smaller relatives, the murres and puffins, and for gulls, gannets, and cormorants, home was land, but food came from the sea. So it is for walruses, seals,

29

Martin Heade's canvas, Approaching Storm *(above), shows the rocky and often-forbidding New England coast as it must have looked to early explorers. The offshore waters were filled with dolphins; those pictured at left were caught, and later drawn, by Benjamin Latrobe on a voyage to America in 1796.*

and polar bears, and to a certain extent, for human beings also. The interplay between sea and land goes on endlessly, hour by hour, minute by minute, forever regulated by the rhythm of the tides.

Grand Manan Island, which lies between New Brunswick and Nova Scotia, provides a dramatic exhibit of this interplay. Here the tidal swell that follows the pull of the moon across the Atlantic rushes into the Bay of Fundy and piles up in a dead end. The sea surges up the cliffs to a height of fifty feet; when the tide suddenly ebbs, the water drops as though the bottom of the sea had fallen out.

On the cliffs of Grand Manan is a luxurious vertical wilderness of seaweeds between the high and low watermarks. These remarkable plants have no roots, for there is no soil on the surface of the tide-washed rocks. Instead, they are equipped with suction disks and tough holdfasts by which they cling to the rocks, defying the pounding of the surf. There are no rigid cells in seaweeds. They shed the force of the water by bending before it, dodging and waving and flexing in the swirling waters.

Among the seaweed jungles are countless pools teeming with secret life. Starfish, crabs, limpets, barnacles, and sea anemones, small and often weirdly beautiful, lead a quiet life now submerged, now half-exposed among the rocky cracks and crevices and the green curtains of seaweed.

At the head of the bay, low tide ex-

poses an expanse of mud, its entire surface twinkling with tiny bubbles blown by countless clams, shrimps, worms, and other creatures as they hastily burrow downward to keep wet and safe until the incoming tide rolls over them again. Crabs scamper in every direction, panicked by the shadows of hundreds of noisy gulls swooping and squawking overhead.

Much of America's northeast coast is bordered by steep cliffs and jumbled rocks, with a stockade of dark evergreen forest looming above. Farther south the rocks give way to sandy lowlands covered with open forests of scrubby oak and pine. Here and there

This engraving of John White's map of the North Carolina Outer Banks shows the "lost colony" on Roanoke Island (left center). White left 100 colonists there in 1587; by his return in 1590, they had vanished.

are sunken regions from which the ocean has withdrawn, leaving cypress swamps and boggy areas where square miles of tall grasses and reeds ripple like sea waves in the wind. The wilderness of the Atlantic coast reflects the play of colors from sea and sky like a kaleidoscope; it vibrates to the thunder of the surf and responds to the rhythm of wind and tide.

There are places where evolution seems to have stood still. Monsters

32

from an ancient age occasionally crawl over the Cape Hatteras sandbars as their ancestors did eons ago. These great loggerhead turtles, weighing as much as five hundred pounds, dredge themselves out of the deep and shuffle heavily across the beach. Crowds of gulls, terns, and sandpipers pay the giant reptiles little attention; only a few, looking bored, step aside to give them a clear way into the grass of the dunes.

West of the Outer Banks' dunes is Pamlico Sound, a gathering place for countless numbers of birds. In its thousands of acres of marshes, sea oats grow ten feet high; thickets of wax myrtle, holly, and cedar are heavy with berries; and spike rushes bursting with seeds grow far out into the shallow water. These vast salt meadows, twenty miles from the mainland, are still a refuge for seabirds, as they were in the primeval wilderness. There, eggs and fledglings are safe from alligators, weasels, bears, and predatory human beings.

The green and white ribbon of the Outer Banks, two hundred miles long and surrounded by blue water, is a haven along the flyways of millions of strong-winged migrating birds. Here is a winter home for snow geese from the Arctic tundra, Canada geese and black ducks from the shores of Hudson Bay, and multitudes of royal terns, laughing gulls, cormorants, gannets, loons, herons, egrets, and bitterns, many of whose summer homes are as far north as the Arctic circle.

Farther south, where the shore meets the Gulf of Mexico, the land slopes so gently down to the sea that the coastline disappears into a vast labyrinth of swamps. Near the tip of Florida lie the mangrove jungles, in one of the most bewildering and treacherous corners of the coastal wilderness. The Spaniards who discovered it, instead of touching land, found themselves lost in a watery maze. Their oars were tripped and their boats caught in tangles of mangrove roots. These mangroves, standing in salt water, use their roots as stilts. Their boat-shaped seedlings drop off and sail away until they run aground, where they take root, grow up and down at the same time, and eventually there is another tree on stilts in this weird forest.

A little farther inland, the mangrove labyrinth merges into the fantastic caldron of life called the Everglades. Although men speak of it as a swamp—awesome with great, gloomy trees, poisonous snakes, and huge alligators—its waters are not stagnant. They are part of a seventy-mile-wide river whose current creeps slowly for a hundred miles through tall, waving saw grass. This grass has blades as sharp-edged as glass, and cuts flesh at the merest touch. In the river of the Everglades are islands, called hummocks, covered with tall trees from which long gray beards of Spanish moss sway slowly back and forth. From a distance the hummocks look like square-riggers under full sail.

Platano. or Planten.

A llagatto. This being but one moneth old was 3. foote
4. ynches in length. and lyue in water.

John White's water colors, painted while he was at the Roanoke Island colony in the 1580's, are among the first pictures
of the New World's plant and animal life. He had probably
seen plantain, a banana-like fruit (upper left), and the pine-
apple (above) in the West Indies. The box tortoise, the graceful flamingo, and the month-old "Allagatto" pictured below
were commonly found along the southern coast of America.

Rising above the babble of wilderness sounds is the blood-curdling screech of the limpkin, a bird that skips across the tops of the swaying grasses, seeking the juicy snails that have climbed up to escape from snapping turtles. The Everglades has another voice, a rumble like distant thunder that seems to come from no particular direction but fills the air. This is the booming of the bull alligator, a creature out of the Age of Reptiles that still lives in slow-moving streams and swamps.

In 1773, William Bartram, a gentle, observant naturalist from Philadelphia, penetrated so deeply into the jungle wilderness of Florida that even his Seminole Indian guide, to whom Florida was home, deserted him. Bartram's curiosity about the wonders he was seeing—wonders he would describe in his journal with precision and poetry—drove him on alone. He traveled in a frail Indian canoe, and more than once he was nearly upset by alligators as they tried to swamp his craft and drag him into the water.

One evening he took shelter under a huge live oak on one of the high hummocks, and there he witnessed something straight out of the age of the "terrible lizards"—a fight between two enormous bull alligators.

"Behold him rushing forth," Bartram wrote. "His enormous body swells. His plaited tail, brandished high, floats upon the lake. The waters like a cataract descend from his opening jaws. Clouds of smoke issue from his dilated nostrils. The earth trembles with his thunder. . . . From the opposite coast of the lagoon, emerges from the deep his rival champion. They suddenly dart upon each other. The boiling surface of the lake marks their rapid course, and a terrible conflict commences. They now sink to the bottom folded together in horrid wreaths. The water becomes thick and discolored. Again they rise, their jaws clap together, re-echoing through the deep surrounding forests. Again they sink, the contest ends at the muddy bottom of the lake, and the vanquished makes a hazardous escape, hiding himself in the muddy turbulent waters and sedge on a distant shore. The proud victor, exulting, returns to the place of action. The shores and forests resound to his dreadful roar, together with the triumphing shouts of the plaited tribes around, witnesses of the horrid combat."

The coral islands called the Florida Keys form a crescent two hundred miles long from the southern tip of Florida into the Gulf of Mexico. Many ships of the early Spanish explorers piled up on the sticky, coral beaches of the Keys. But the Spaniards also reaped harvests of birds' eggs. When Audubon, the great bird artist, visited

OVERLEAF: *A French map of the Gulf coast wilderness about 1750 includes the Mississippi River (far left) and Pensacola (lower right). The squares are Indian towns. Also shown are a rattlesnake, an alligator, and, at lower left, a "chat sauvage" (wildcat).*

ILLINOIS

PAYS DES CHI-

PAYS DES

Nota. La nation des
chaimes est très Nombreuse et elle a
guerre très souvent avec les chicanhas, ils
sont chasseurs, naiment point les villages sur les eaux
ils habitent dans les prairies, et sont amis des françois
pour du traité ou Marchandises.

Chacchoue
Yazoa
ARCANSAS

NATCHÉS

LAC

LAC

LAC

Chat sauvage au bord du Lac
Mer ils ne nourissent que d'huitres
ou de poissons

PASCAG

Biloxy

Baye du
Biloxy

GOLPHE   DU

CA CHI CTAS

Cette nation des chicachas est très dangereuse elle
occupe les montagnes et les prairies, elle est belligueuse
a guette avec les chactas et autres nations est elle qui
a entré chez elles les anglais et par Mr de
Bienville y fut sur eux en 1736 et n'y a
rien fait que de perte du Monde, et aussi
dépense bien du bien pour n'avoir pas
une seule chose sure.

Fort du chicachas

CARTE
DE LA
Province
DE LA
Louissianne

CHACTAS

Le Lac

Serpent à sonnettes très dangereux
car qu'il a d'espece de grelots à la
il autant d'années

La Riv Roy

Le Lac

MOBI LIENS

Appalaches

Baye de l'Isle
Dauphine

MINISTERE DE LA GUERRE
ARCHIVES
DES CARTES.
DEPOT DE LA GUERRE.

MEXIQUE

Bird Key in 1832, he watched a single cargo of sooty tern and noddy tern eggs, weighing eight tons, being loaded aboard a Cuban boat. In 1928 Bird Key mysteriously started to sink, and it vanished in a hurricane ten years later.

The persecution of the wonderful birds of the Keys reduced their population to a small fraction of what it was when that wilderness was in its prime. Then in 1908 the Dry Tortugas, the most remote islands of the Keys, became a bird sanctuary. A census by the National Park Service has put the number of tern nests on those islands at around 85,000 in recent years. When nature is not interfered with, she is quick to regenerate her wilderness.

Today a highway runs for 150 miles across forty coral islands from Miami to Key West. It passes many remnants of the only wilderness in the continental United States with tropical trees. Coconut palms lean over the beaches. Thickets of sea grapes have amazingly twisted branches and wide leaves with blood-red veins; strangler figs choke the trees they climb on; and the monstrous gumbo limbo sends out horizontal branches that billow like huge fire hoses. Here is mastic with its acid olives, mahogany like that in the Amazon valley, and sapodilla, the chewing-gum tree whose sap turns to chicle. A few colorful tree snails are still to be found among the branches of these trees. In a few places Key deer, the size of slender little dogs, still make their trails in scattered groves.

West of Florida, the Gulf of Mexico touches a different sort of coastal wilderness, where the salt sea seems to change into another sea of undulating grass and reeds. The first white man to set foot on the northern shores of the Gulf of Mexico barely lived to tell the tale.

In 1528 a Spanish conquistador named Cabeza de Vaca was shipwrecked off what is now the coast of Texas. He and thirty-nine companions, the only survivors of an ill-starred Spanish expedition that had set out to explore the Gulf coast, crawled up on a sandbar, naked, famished, ready to die. They were picked up by some wretched Indians who had come from the interior to dig roots for food. They made de Vaca their slave, and until he made his escape four years later, he was forced to wade into the swamps along the coast to dig up the roots of the reeds that grew there. It was torture. "My fingers were so worn," he wrote, "that they bled if a straw touched them, and the reeds, many of which were broken, tore my flesh . . ."

The source of the reed ocean along the coasts of Texas and Louisiana is the Mississippi River delta, formed of silt carried south from the face of half the continent. As this endless cargo of soil reaches the continental shelf, it meets with waves and ocean currents that carry it along the shore to form a chain of barrier islands. Behind the sand dunes that are built up on the seaward side grow acres of tall grasses, their roots anchored in the fertile sediment, their tops shifting like waves. This wilderness, created by the action and counteraction of the river and the sea, never stops growing. Since de Vaca first saw it, twenty-five cubic miles of sediment have been added.

In his misery, de Vaca saw this wilderness as a plague spot of storms, extremes of heat and cold, mosquitoes, and near-starvation. But there is, as well, wonder and beauty here. Blue waterways, teeming with fish, run among the endless stretches of towering reeds. Countless islands support little jungles of cypress and palmetto, crisscrossed by the trails of deer, bear, muskrat, and hordes of rats, mice, and other small animals. Countless mudholes are the hide-outs of turtles, snakes, salamanders, and frogs. Here are magnificent refuges for swans, geese, ducks, and some of the most beautiful wading birds of the American wilderness. Here the whooping cranes, tallest of American birds, have their wintering grounds.

The American wilderness holds no event of greater wonder than when millions of birds of many kinds appear as if by magic out of the reeds and head north in the spring. Then the sky is laced with formations of waterfowl. The endless flocks weave skeins across the continent, linking the wild, open tundra and dark woods of the north with this hiding place in the southern coastal wilderness of swaying reeds.

Exploring the Florida Everglades in 1773, naturalist William Bartram sketched an "alligator hole" (above), a spring where the huge reptiles hunted for fish. His drawing below of a pair of bull alligators was made on the St. Johns River.

39

3

A Forest Primeval

The Pilgrims who saw the coast of Massachusetts from the deck of the *Mayflower* in 1620 must have had mixed feelings. Here was land for their "free possessing and enjoying thereof," but it looked very strange and bleak.

They were not the first English people to land on the New England coast. A twenty-three-year-old adventurer named Martin Pring explored the rocky northern shoreline in 1603. Captain George Weymouth brought a party to Monhegan Island, on the coast of Maine, and spent the summer of 1605 in the Boothbay Harbor area. The reports they brought back to England filled the Pilgrims with expectations of a sunny, flowering land.

In their descriptions everything was green: "Firre, Birch, Oke, and Beech, as farre as we saw along the shore. . . . On the verge grow Gooseberries, Strawberries, Wild pease, and Wild rose bushes." They spoke of "beauty and goodness . . . that did so ravish us with variety of pleasantnesse that we could not tell what to command but only admire."

But Pring and Weymouth had seen the eastern woodlands only in the freshness of spring and the ripeness

Pioneers seeking new land in Kentucky followed the Wilderness Road through Cumberland Gap in the Appalachians. Painted here by George Caleb Bingham, Daniel Boone leads a party through the gap in 1775.

of summer. The Pilgrims, on the other hand, made their landfall at the low, sandy tip of Cape Cod in the month of November. When they brought the *Mayflower* across the bay to Plymouth there was a foot of snow on the ground. The trunks of the big trees looked as though they were made of iron. The green, leafy roof of summer had crumbled and fallen, to lie buried under the snow.

The forest not only looked strange and mournful, but it was haunted with ghostly sounds. On a cold night, with the leaves off the trees, sounds carry a long way. One of the sounds the Pilgrims heard in the dead of night was the deep, drawn-out, throaty howl of the great gray timber wolf. Starting on a low note, it would soar higher, becoming thinner and sharper until it ended with a wailing shriek that made the blood run cold.

Another sound that carried far in the night across the winter wilderness was the barking of a fox. A mile away, another fox would answer; as the two foxes barked back and forth, others would join in the long-distance conversation. The melancholy "whoo, whoo, whoo" of the great horned owl was heard, and there were the faraway screams of the cougar and the wildcat which, in the silence that followed, seemed doubly treacherous.

Every creature that stays awake in this snowbound wilderness has its own secret of survival. The wolf, fox,

BOSTON ATHENAEUM

Martin Pring was the first to explore closely the Massachusetts coast. At left, his party lands at Plymouth harbor in 1603, with mastiffs as protection against hostile Indians. The palm trees are pure imagination.

The Natural Bridge of Virginia, painted at right in 1824 by an officer of the British Royal Navy, is one of the wonders of the eastern wilderness. The 215-foot arch is on property once owned by Thomas Jefferson.

and bobcat are heavily furred. They do not depend on plant food, but are meat-eaters that live in midwinter by pursuing other smaller animals or digging up and killing those asleep under the snow. As for the cougar, one whitetail deer a week can see that great cat through the winter.

For the deer themselves, the buds on trees and bushes, to which other animals pay no attention, are a perfect winter food. The buds are there by the millions, at a height well above the snow but within easy reach of the long-necked, long-legged whitetail. But many other animals go into hiding when the leaves fall. The woodchuck crawls into its burrow and curls up on a bed of grass. The chipmunk is snug in its tunnel on a mattress of grasses and dead leaves, atop a winter store of acorns, nuts, and seeds on which it nibbles drowsily from time to time.

In the den of the black bear, the she-bear's cubs are born while she half-sleeps. Cold weather sends the raccoon into a hole high up in a hollow tree, where it will sleep for as long as two months—though a January thaw may bring it out to look for something to eat. Likewise, the skunk disappears into his long underground tunnel, but mild weather in midwinter may wake him up, and it will take zero temperatures to send him back to sleep again.

Indeed, every corner of that wilderness is filled with sleeping life. The eggs of insects under stones, twigs, and leaves; ladybird beetles in the cracks of fallen trees; snails in holes in the ground or under stones; snakes in tunnels under the forest floor; spiders drowsing in the silken bags they have spun; tree frogs under rotting logs or leaves; snapping turtles encased in mud—they all wait out the cold in the stillness of the sleeping wilderness.

Then, as the months pass and the days lengthen, the winter sleep comes to an end. The snow melts and sap rises in the trunks of the trees. From leaf buds myriads of tiny flowerlets pop suddenly into bloom. These tree flowers of the eastern woodlands are so small and come and go so quickly that they are not often noticed; many people do not realize that elms, maples, and oaks have flowers. They tint the tops of red maples with crimson. Elms are flushed with purple, and the flowers of sugar maple, oak, and ash are a yellow-green mist.

While these tree flowers are in

Although John James Audubon is best known for his paintings of animals and birds, he also collected specimens of American insects to sell to the British Museum. This page from a sketchbook he made in the early 1820's includes an emperor butterfly (upper right), a grasshopper (second row, left), and a yellow-winged wood cockroach (bottom left).

44

bloom, the spring sun pours warmth into the leaf-mold on the forest floor. It is then that the wild flowers suddenly appear. They spring up between fallen leaves and twigs, urged upward by the pull of the sunlight, and spread a tinted carpet underneath the trees. For thousands of years before white men discovered them and gave them names, they had been a part of the springtime pageant of the eastern wilderness—trailing arbutus, hepatica, bloodroot; violet, trillium, and jack-in-the-pulpit; starflower, columbine, bleeding heart.

With the coming of the leaves, the nesting birds arrive. In the leafless days of winter the branches had been bare of birds, except for an occasional congregation of crows or a saucy bluejay, a drilling woodpecker or a cheerful chickadee. Most birds had gone south with the falling of the leaves. Now they come back—the tanagers and the orioles, the thrushes, thrashers, and wood warblers, the robins, bluebirds, and buntings. The summer homes of many of them are basket nests, built snugly within a canopy of leaves, pleasantly lighted with a sun-flecked glow, and suspended out of reach of animals prowling the forest.

This summer wilderness is packed with life. Thickets of alder, hazelnut, and blueberry are the hiding places of countless animals. A fallen oak is a favorite harbor for grouse in a storm; there they are safe from the wind, and from foxes as well. Holes in trees become apartments for owls, raccoons, and squirrels. A tree struck by lightning or half-killed by disease is a boon to the wild bees that swarm in and fill it with honeycomb. The tree-climbing black bear thinks so too, as he dips in a paw and licks it off, eating the bees along with the honey as though they were raisins.

The darkness underneath a fallen log hides the tunnel openings to the houses of a hundred white-footed mice. A blanket of green moss grows over the log, and ferns and mushrooms spring from its rotting crevices; decay gives birth to new life in the never-ending cycle of the wilderness.

So it was in the eastern woodlands where the Pilgrims built their colony, and so it is today in the woodlands that remain. The original virgin forests, except for a few small, scattered tracts, were all cut long ago.

These were forests where the natural life cycle of the trees had never been

Its profusion of birds made the eastern wilderness a wonderland for naturalists. Mark Catesby sketched the bald eagle (top left) and the Carolina parakeet (bottom right) in 1722. The belted kingfisher (top right) was drawn by John Abbot in Georgia in 1827. William Bartram painted the green bittern (bottom left). Passenger pigeons (center), once the most numerous of American birds, are extinct.

interrupted by settlers or loggers. As a result, trees grew to enormous size. Their high branches obscured the sun from the forest floor, so that over great tracts of woodland there was little underbrush as we know it, only a thick mat of fallen leaves and nuts where the wild animals had a continual supply of food. Early settlers found few singing birds in the great virgin forests—they came only as fields were cleared and grain was sown.

Men of the seventeenth and eighteenth centuries could read the nature of soil and the presence of water by the kind of trees that grew. They could look at forested land and know which groves to clear for the best crops. William Byrd of Virginia, who surveyed the dividing line between Virginia and North Carolina in 1728, noted in his journal that "the soil where the locust thicket grew was exceedingly rich, as it constantly is where that kind of tree is naturally and largely produced." Dr. Joseph Doddridge, who wrote about western Virginia in the late eighteenth century, tells of the hunter predicting the presence of a river, "by seeing large ash, bass-wood, and sugar trees, beautifully festooned with large grape vines."

The virgin forest was magnificent, but it could also be monotonous and terribly lonely. As late as 1913, a Maine guide and hunter named Joseph Knowles went into the northern Maine woods on a bet, without provisions, clothes, or tools, to see

Wildcats used to be common in eastern forests. This engraving, of a cat attacking a stag, is from the journal of an Englishman who toured the Carolinas in the 1700's.

LAWSON, *History of Carolina*, 1718

if he could survive for two months.

Physically he found it fairly easy, for he was a trained woodsman. He said that his worst problem was the suffering caused by loneliness—that, and the awful monotony of the deep forest. He wrote, "True monotony means a tree and a tree and a tree, and then some more of the same kind of trees over and over again."

Eighteenth-century hunters spent months in the virgin wilderness until its freedom and its loneliness became a way of life to them. But they usually hunted in pairs, not only for companionship but for safety. William Byrd described the kind of terrain the explorer or hunter could run into when he talked about the Dismal Swamp of

Virginia, where his surveying party took fifteen days to go nine miles.

"Since the surveyors had entered the Dismal [Swamp]," Byrd wrote, "they had laid eyes on no living creature: neither bird nor beast, insect nor reptile came in view. Doubtless, the eternal shade that broods over this mighty bog, and hinders the sunbeams from blessing the ground, makes it an uncomfortable habitation for anything that has life. . . . Not even a turkey buzzard will venture to fly over it."

Gradually the trees of the eastern woodland were cleared. Farms were planted and swamps were drained. The great supply of virgin timber was used up wastefully to make houses, as if that supply were boundless. One of the fastest ways of clearing was to "girdle" the trees by cutting the bark away in a ring so that the spring sap could not rise. By this method great tracts of trees died and were felled each summer.

The eastern woodlands of today, covering less than one-fifth of what was once forest, are practically all second growth. A continuous band of cities and factories runs along the eastern seaboard from Boston southward as far as Maryland. Inland are farms, orchards, vineyards, and more cities for mile after mile in what was once nearly unbroken forest. It is no wonder that as the human population expanded, the wild population shrank. In the east the fox, the black bear, the raccoon, and a host of smaller animals can be seen if one knows where to look for them. The birds still return to nest wherever there are trees, and wherever there are woods, there are usually also deer.

But for many other creatures it is a different story. The cougar is about gone from the eastern woodlands. The wolf has vanished not only from the east but very nearly from the western wilderness as well. To hear the deep, drawn-out wolf's howl as the Pilgrims heard it, it is necessary to travel west into the wilds along the Canadian border.

Gone, too, is the gobbling commotion of the wild turkey, a common sound in Pilgrim times. In those days great numbers of these big-bodied, long-necked, small-headed birds, with their splendid bronze plumage, strutted in clearings or perched silhouetted against the sky in the tops of trees. They were seldom molested by wolves, foxes, or predatory birds. But the cougars knew how good turkey-meat was—and so did the Indians, and so the white men also soon found out. Between unlimited hunting and the cutting of the virgin forests, the wild turkeys disappeared from all but a few out-of-the-way southern forests. There are other birds of the eastern

OVERLEAF: *Samuel Finley Breese Morse, a renowned artist before he achieved greater fame as the inventor of the telegraph, painted Niagara Falls in 1835. Even then it was a tourist attraction. The view is from the Canadian side of the Niagara River.*

woodlands that can never be brought back; like the great auk, they are gone forever.

Of these vanished birds the most numerous were the passenger pigeons. White men who saw the eastern woodlands in their prime told remarkable stories of these strong-winged travelers. New Englander John Josselyn wrote in the seventeenth century of an airy army of pigeons with "neither beginning nor ending, length nor breadth, and so thick I could see no Sun." In the words of a later writer, a flock "like some great river sweeping at sixty miles per hour, reaching a deep valley . . . would pour its living mass headlong down hundreds of feet, sounding as though a whirlwind was abroad in the land."

It was partly this habit of staying together that led to the passenger pigeons' doom. Instead of nesting in scattered pairs like their cousins the mourning doves, or in family groups like turkeys, quail, and grouse, they nested in crowds, and in crowds they flew in search of the acorns, nuts, and seeds on which they fed. As the forests shrank, the overcrowding grew; there were fewer flocks of pigeons, but those flocks became more spectacular. In 1878, a flock numbering tens of millions nested near Petoskey, Michigan. It was the last great flock ever seen. By 1914, the last remaining passenger pigeon, a captive in a Cincinnati zoo, was dead.

How did it happen? The answer is quite simple. Like the great auks, pas-senger pigeons were good eating and easy to kill, and there were men who were delighted to do the killing. They were slaughtered by the millions and shipped by the barrelful to the cities. Laws to protect the birds and prevent the slaughter were passed, but they were passed too late.

Farther south lived a very different bird, the Carolina parakeet, but its story is strangely like the story of the passenger pigeon. In fact, the last of its kind, also a captive bird, died in that same year of 1914. Carolina parakeets were gorgeously colored creatures whose feathers were used to trim ladies' hats. Others were captured to be sold as cage birds. To orchard owners they were a nuisance; to hunters, an irresistible target.

"At Big Bone Lick, thirty miles above the mouth of the Kentucky River," wrote Alexander Wilson, the first great American ornithologist, "I saw them in great numbers. They came screaming through the woods in the morning, about an hour after sunrise. . . . When they alighted on the ground, it appeared at a distance as if covered by a carpet of richest green, orange, and yellow: they afterwards settled in one body, on a neighboring tree, which stood detached from any other, covering almost every twig of it." They were easy to kill, and so they dwindled. Now the Carolina parakeet, too, is gone.

For yet another bird of the southern forests the story is somewhat different, but the ending is no less melancholy. A magnificent flying creature, the ivory-billed woodpecker, lived in a hidden empire of swamps and bottomland. Here and there on the mucky floor, among soggy moss-covered fallen trunks, the black mirrors of ponds reflected the white and gold blossoms of waterlilies. It was a gloomy, ancient place where gray Spanish moss trailed from dead and decaying trees.

Upon these trees the ivory-billed woodpecker depended for its livelihood. A twenty-inch green-black bird banded with white and crested with red, it had a powerful beak which looked like a dagger made of ivory. Its only food consisted of grubs dug from under the bark of dying trees.

To keep alive, every pair of ivory-bills needed about six square miles of swampy wilderness. As the swamps were drained and the dead and dying trees cleared away, there was no space left for them. It is barely possible, some people believe, that a few of them may still exist in some remote southern swamp, but the chance is slight.

The tide of civilization was held back for nearly two centuries from much of the eastern woodlands by a mountain frontier. This is the Appalachian Highlands forming a huge wall west of the coastal plain from New England to Alabama.

In 1670, John Lederer, one of the first Europeans to explore this barrier, saw the Blue Ridge range stretching west to the horizon. Blue-green moun-

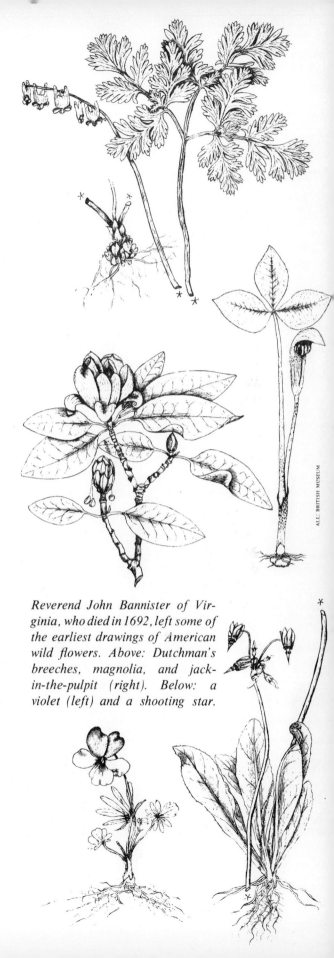

ALL: BRITISH MUSEUM

Reverend John Bannister of Virginia, who died in 1692, left some of the earliest drawings of American wild flowers. Above: Dutchman's breeches, magnolia, and jack-in-the-pulpit (right). Below: a violet (left) and a shooting star.

54

tains rose higher and higher in the distance, with no sign of a gap through them. Virginians called them "the Endless Mountains," and so they seemed, except to unsung and unrecorded hunters who followed narrow Indian traces through them. A year after Lederer's return, a Captain Thomas Batts crossed the high dividing line, where the rivers flowed west instead of east, and explored the New River, which still winds through wild green woods and forbidding rock cliffs. He and his companions found trees that had already been carved with English names.

On August 29, 1716, the first large-scale expedition set out to explore the Blue Ridge. These "Knights of the Golden Horseshoe" were led by Alexander Spotswood, the royal governor of Virginia. On that morning he was dressed in green velvet riding clothes and Russian leather boots, and wore a fine plumed hat. One of the gentlemen who rode with him was a young ensign from the British army named John Fontaine. According to Fontaine's account, the expedition not only endured but enjoyed the rough passage in true cavalier spirit. Their provisions included a large stock of wine, rum, and champagne.

One of the worst hazards of the

Settlers found they could most easily turn forestland into farmland by "girdling" the trees—cutting out a ring of bark to kill them, making them easier to chop down and burn. This water color dates from the 1840's.

virgin mountain woodlands were the acres of dense laurel thickets. "We came to a thicket so tightly laced together," Fontaine wrote, "that we had a great deal of trouble to get through; our baggage was injured, our clothes torn to rags, and the saddles and holsters also torn." Nor were laurel thickets their only problem. All through his diary Fontaine recorded the killing of huge rattlesnakes.

After eight days of cutting its way through the mountains, the party halted on one of the highest peaks of the Blue Ridge. Below them lay the beautiful, untouched valley of the Shenandoah, which they named the Euphrates after the river where the Garden of Eden is traditionally placed.

They stopped at a tiny mountain spring, one of the headwaters of the James River. "There," said Fontaine, "we drank the King's health in champagne and fired a volley, the Princess's health in Burgundy and fired a volley, and all the rest of the Royal Family in Claret and fired a volley." Fontaine took time out from the merrymaking to note that "about a musket shot from the spring there is another which rises and runs down the other side. It goes westward."

The waters of that stream eventually reached the great Mississippi watershed. Beyond the Mississippi lay a new wilderness, one of the most alien that Americans were to discover and learn to live in—the prairie slope.

4

The Prairie Slope

Woodsmen find direction by the way the water flows and the moss grows. Sailors trace their course by the stars. The Americans who explored the western prairie in the nineteenth century described what they found in terms of the sea, for it was the only thing they knew that resembled this strange land.

When Major Stephen Long led an expedition over the prairie in 1820, in his party was a young physician and botanist, Dr. Edwin James. Dr. James wrote that "broken flying clouds . . . coursing rapidly over the plain, seemed to put the whole in motion, and we appeared to ourselves as if riding on the unquiet billows of the ocean."

Covered wagons, slowly rolling across the wide expanse, were called "prairie schooners." Later, cowboys driving cattle north set a wagon tongue toward the North Star at night for direction in the next day's travel, steering by the stars as if they were mariners.

The prairie is actually one long, gradual slope. From the western bank of the Mississippi River, where the land is a few feet above sea level, it climbs upward until it meets the

In Alfred Jacob Miller's 1837 painting, a fur-trading caravan plods across the shimmering, sun-baked western plains near the forks of the Platte River. The region was scorned as a wasteland by early explorers.

ramparts of the Rocky Mountains.

Lieutenant Zebulon Pike experienced, rather than saw, this slope when he set out from St. Louis in July, 1806, with a detachment of army troops and a party of Osage and Pawnee Indians to find a pass through the Rocky Mountains. From July on into the wild prairie winter they traveled, following the Arkansas River, then Indian and Spanish trails. On November 15 Pike wrote in his journal: "At two o'clock in the afternoon I thought I could distinguish a mountain to our right, which appeared like a small blue cloud. . . ." It was the first view of the mountain later to be known as Pike's Peak, a landmark for thousands of settlers.

Having weathered a prairie snowstorm which plunged the thermometer to 17 degrees below zero, Pike and the expedition's doctor took the altitude of the peak. They calculated it at 10,581 feet from the prairie, and "admitting that the prairie was 8,000 feet from the level of the sea," decided that the peak was 18,581 feet high. Pike's estimate was somewhat off—the base of Pike's Peak is really about 5,000 feet above sea level—but in reaching it he had climbed a mile high up the long slope from St. Louis. Still, the prairie is so vast that to a man looking out across its grassy expanse it appears as level as a great, undulating inland sea.

And a sea, in fact, is just what it once was. It became dry land perhaps 100 million years ago, when the great body of water that geologists call the Cretaceous Sea, extending all the way from the Arctic to the Gulf of Mexico, gradually withdrew. At its western edge, about the same time, the earth's crust began to fold upward, producing the Rocky Mountains.

Since then, bit by bit, the rains of millions of years have been wearing down the jagged peaks, gradually carrying their upper surfaces down to the plain. Over those millions of years, endless stream-borne loads of gravel, sand, and clay have spread out over the lowlands, building them up into a great tilted tableland.

The earliest European to glimpse the prairie—or at least its southern edge—was Cabeza de Vaca, the shipwrecked Spanish adventurer. Two centuries were to pass before Chevalier de La Vérendrye, a Frenchman, entered deeply into the region.

The year was 1742. After traveling the Canadian fur routes as far west as Lake Superior, Vérendrye struck off to the southwest, lured by the old hope that the waters of the Pacific might be just over the horizon. But he found instead a sea of grass, a thing utterly bewildering to a man accustomed to paddling along lakes and streams and following forest trails. The Indians he encountered spoke of

Sprinkled with imaginary landmarks and unknown Indian tribes, this fanciful map of the Mississippi River was painted in Spain at the end of the 17th century. The artist based most of his geography on rumor.

MAPPA · DEL · RIO · MISSISIPI

a tribe of "horse Indians" to the west. Horses? This rumor from across the prairie intrigued Vérendrye. Indians could have gotten horses only from the Spaniards; thus the Gulf of California must lie somewhere beyond the sea of grass.

So the Chevalier and his brother plodded on and on through "barren country with no trees, and burning sun." Finally, on January 1, 1743, along what is now the Montana-Wyoming border, they saw in the dim distance mountains jutting against the sky like a mirage. Their Indian guides refused to continue. These first white men to see the Rockies turned and made their way back across the limitless, frigid prairie to the Great Lakes country, where there was game among the forest shadows, and campfires could be made beside lakes that reflected the stars.

Soldier-explorers sent to map the far west in the early years of the nineteenth century had little good to say

Major Stephen Long's party is shown parleying with a band of Pawnee Indians along the Missouri River in 1819, during the first stage of its prairie explorations. Samuel Seymour, the official artist of the expedition, sketched this scene.

about the sea of grass. Major Long labeled the region east of the Rockies the Great American Desert. Lieutenant Pike was of the same opinion. A young Englishman named George Frederick Ruxton, who came looking for high adventure in the west, reported, "No scenery in nature is more dreary and monotonous than the aspect of the grand prairies . . . a vast, undulating, expansive arid waste. . . . The sky is generally overcast and storms sweep incessantly over the bare plains. . . ."

In order to conquer the prairie, men had to learn to live its way. In the eastern woodlands, once the trees were down, the farms planted, and the towns formed, Americans could impose the way of living they had known before. But there was no way to do this in a sea of grass. The silence, the distance, and the weather required a new kind of physical and mental endurance.

Pike's 1806 journal describes the toll of the prairie winter on the bodies and minds of his men. January 17: "The feet of nine of our [sixteen] men were frozen." January 18: "Hungry and without cover." January 19: "extremely weak and faint, it being the fourth day since we had received sustenance. . . . We were marching hard. . . ." On January 24 Pike wrote, ". . . for the first time I heard a man express himself in a seditious manner. He exclaimed that 'it was more than human nature could bear to march . . . without sustenance, through snows

three feet deep, and carry burdens only fit for horses, etc.'" The prairie's blazing, arid summer exacted an equal toll. Winter or summer, the endless, open space was a terror to many.

It took the American people generations of knowing and living on the prairie to see it as something more than a dreary wasteland. The writer Washington Irving, who went there in the 1830's, was one of the first to be pleased with what he saw. Mounted on a fast horse, he galloped after bison and discovered the exhilaration and beauty of this different sort of wilderness.

The eastern frontier of the prairie that Irving saw ran along an irregular forest margin extending in places to what is now Indiana, and northward diagonally across Wisconsin and into Canada. As far west as the Dakotas and central Kansas, it was a lush region of tall, bluestem grass. The landscape was rolling and graceful, the grass bending before the wind.

Among the grass bloomed a multicolored succession of prairie flowers —pale-blue pasqueflowers in early spring, followed by the bright pink of prairie phlox, the pale yellow, pink, and white of enormous evening primroses, the golden yellow of the towering compass-plant, the crimson of milkweeds, the purple of blazing stars.

The lower, moist places near creeks and sloughs were little oases where cattails, dwarf willows, and blue flags grew. Countless water-loving birds had nesting places in the marshy

cover—red-winged and yellow-headed blackbirds, mallards, coots, rails, and bitterns. By day, the calling of bob-whites, the bubbling songs of marsh wrens, the lisping notes of marsh-dwelling yellowthroats, and the liquid voices of meadowlarks filled the air. The nights were loud with the trilling of multitudes of frogs.

It was in this rich, moist, rustling wilderness that the prairie chickens congregated on spring evenings to carry on the strange ritual of their courtship. The booming sounds they made could be heard everywhere. And it was here that one of the grandest and weirdest spectacles in nature took place—the dances of the cranes.

The gray sandhill cranes danced in flocks—running, pacing, flapping,

bugling, a hundred or a thousand birds at a time. The statelier, more solitary whooping cranes danced in pairs, silently bowing to each other, flapping their great, dazzling, black-tipped wings, springing into the air, leaping over each other as if in a ballet. These dances were a kind of marriage ceremony. Afterward, somewhere among the cattails and bul-

The western prairie—"beautiful, unbroken by bush or rock; unspoiled by plow or spade"—was painted by a 19th-century artist named William Hart. In his day, an observant man could count a wide variety of wildlife during a short journey over the rolling grassland.

63

rushes of a prairie marsh, a nest was built, eggs were laid, and the fluffy chicks were hatched.

By fall, as the days grew shorter and the nights colder, birds were everywhere on the move. Flocks of Canada geese, southbound from their nesting-places to the north, honked overhead, sometimes alighting to feed and rest for a day or two before moving on. Then one day the whooping cranes were on their way south for the winter, their destination a reed-covered island situated somewhere along the Gulf of Mexico.

Not all the birds migrated. The bobwhites and the prairie chickens stayed on, finding sheltered places where they would huddle on snowy nights to keep warm. Frogs and turtles hid in the mud to sleep the winter through. In dens half-in, half-out of frozen ponds, muskrats were still active. So were the fierce, fast-moving minks and weasels that preyed on them. And so, too, were the sly coyotes, small prairie cousins of the gray timber wolf, barking and wailing in chorus on winter nights. Here roamed the great hump-backed bison. And

GREGG, Commerce of the Prairie. 1844

Vast prairie-dog villages, inhabited as well by snakes and owls, dotted the plains until the early 1900's. Then a widespread poisoning campaign nearly wiped out the grass-eating prairie dogs to preserve grazing land for cattle.

64

here, among the trees at the edges of the streams, the Indian tribes that hunted them—Cree, Sauk, Shawnee— built their fires and pitched their pointed tepees covered with bison hides.

This was the tall-grass prairie of a little over a century ago. It is a very different place today. The bison are reduced to a few herds, and most Indians live on reservations. Whooping cranes are gone from the prairie. Like the ivory-billed woodpeckers, they need space in which to live and nest. As the prairie marshes, one by one, were drained, and the waving sea of tall grass gave way year by year to fields of corn, oats, and clover, and to pastures close-cropped by grazing cattle, there was not enough space left. The few dozen whooping cranes left in the world now fly from a refuge on the Texas coast all the way to northwest Canada to raise their young.

It is the same with the prairie chickens. They are seldom seen any more, and from the region of the tall grass they have gone farther west and south. Indeed, the tall grass itself is almost gone. Except in a few meadows which have never been plowed, other grasses have taken its place; and when the prairie grasses went, many of the prairie flowers went, too. The bright pink of the prairie phlox, once so common, is now a rare sight.

The chief reason for these changes in the tall-grass prairie landscape is that its black soil is perhaps the richest and most fertile in America. From a wilderness it became the Corn Belt, producing grain and meat for much of the rest of the country. It is a tidy and prosperous region of red barns and rolling fields. There are only a few small patches of wilderness here and there, mainly along the streams. What few prairie sloughs are left—and they are rare indeed—are still gathering places for enormous numbers of birds. Blackbirds, meadowlarks, and yellow-throats still sing; the whistling call of the bobwhite can still be heard; and on a spring evening the trilling of the frogs goes on just as it has for ages past.

West of the tall-grass prairie, where the land rises two thousand feet or more above sea level, begins the region known as the Great Plains. Here rain falls less frequently, and the air is drier. It is here that the great solitude of land and sky begins. Instead of bluestem, its 350,000 square miles are covered with grass of another, shorter kind, the buffalo grass.

This plant, a masterpiece of nature, has made the Great Plains unique. It grows only a few inches tall, but its erect, crisp blades are densely crowded. During the millions of years since the uptilting of the Rocky Mountains cut off the moisture-bearing winds from the west, this short grass had been building up a dense root system, ten or twelve feet deep.

When the tall-grass land had all been taken up, farmers moved into the Great Plains, upsetting the natural balance of growth and decay which

Despite their incredible speed, the western pronghorns (above) are not safe from predators. Wily prairie wolves, like the one shown below, will chase a pronghorn in relays until the harassed animal drops from exhaustion. Titian Peale did these water colors in 1819.

had sustained the animals and the Plains Indians. The plow bit into the plains. The danger was forecast by cattlemen, soil experts—and Indians. The farmers paid no attention. Where buffalo grass grew, they thought, so would wheat.

At first the new farms brought such yields of wheat that they were called bonanza farms. North Dakota farmers laughed at a remark an old Sioux Indian made to a Scandinavian named John Christiansen in the spring of 1883. As Christiansen was driving his plow horse over the virgin prairie, turning under the thick buffalo grass and leaving behind him a ribbon of rich, black sod, he realized that he was being watched silently by an Indian. He stopped plowing. The old brave knelt by the turned furrow and plunged his hand into the sod and buried grass. "Wrong side up," he said, and turned and walked away.

Then the droughts came. The precious topsoil, its protective mat of grass roots gone, was lifted by the wind and blown away. What had once been some of the richest soil in America, in an area reaching from northwest Kansas to Texas, was known by 1935 as the Dust Bowl. It became more desolate by far than when Major Long labeled the region the Great American Desert.

Now there is planning in the prairies. Great dams conserve needed water, and there is a marker on Route 10 in North Dakota at the place where the old Sioux gave his warning, so that it will never be forgotten by men who try to tame the short-grass wilderness.

But the sod, that immense underground storehouse of food energy which stayed moist through months of searing winds and freezing blizzards, was gone forever. Gone were the deep roots that kept the grass crop safe when a prairie fire roared over, and that left it unhurt by the trampling hooves and close-nibbling teeth of millions of wandering bison.

The bison, often incorrectly called the buffalo (true buffalo are found only in the Old World), is the greatest of American grazing mammals. Its ancestors came over the Bering land bridge from Asia perhaps 500,000 years ago. Here the bison evolved the kind of teeth needed to bite off and chew the tough prairie grass. It took a great deal of grazing to pack the bulky frame of a bison with life. He had to crop and chew for most of his life, which might last forty years. And he was leisurely and unconcerned about the rest of the world while going about the business of keeping himself fed. He was quick enough on his feet, though, when panicked by a prairie fire. Then he had the speed of a runaway freight engine.

He was too big and too indifferent to hide himself, and the high plains offered few shadows into which an animal could disappear while standing still. A bison breaking the line of the horizon could be seen from afar, and a herd moving across the plains raised a dust cloud that betrayed it

Bison fording the Yellowstone River as a prairie fire rages in the distance provided artist Charles Wimar with this eerie scene. "We were actually terrified at the immense numbers," wrote a witness to such a crossing. "The river was filled . . . with their heads."

for some fifty miles around. But through the ages, until men began arriving—especially men mounted on horses and armed with guns—the bison never had to reckon with another animal.

They had no reason to get mad at anything—anything, that is, except each other. The duel of two bison bulls was a spectacular thing. Under their hooves the prairie sod quivered, and the rumble of their bellowing sounded from a distance like heavy artillery.

The duel began with two animals standing twenty feet apart, working up their wrath, kicking pieces of sod into the air. Suddenly there was a lunge, then a sickening crash as two tons of flesh and bone collided head-on. Then once more the opponents would back away twenty feet, paw the ground, and lunge again. This would continue until one or the other of the bulls was too stunned or too exhausted to fight any longer. It was not often a battle to the death; in any case, the rest of the herd went on grazing, quite unconcerned.

When a man came face to face with an angry bison, he saw two short black horns jutting out of an immense dark mane; round eyes that glowed like flashlights; a mouth gaping open, with the tongue stiffly protruding; and, above his battering-ram of a head, a great hump that quivered with rage.

No one knows just how many bison lived during their long heyday on the Great Plains, but zoologists believe that there may have been as many as 60 million of them.

Long before the coming of the bison, the high plains were already the home of another grazing mammal, the swift and lovely pronghorn. They are probably the fastest-moving of all North American mammals. Having no single spot that they called home, they were forever wandering, racing, and playing tag at speeds of more than forty miles an hour.

Unlike the bison, the pronghorn had to be on guard against animal enemies long before the coming of man. One of these enemies was the coyote. At the least suspicion of coyotes, a signal would be flashed from pronghorn to pronghorn, with the speed of light. And a remarkable kind of signaling it is. Each animal carries in place of a tail a rounded cushion of dense white hairs, rather like a powder puff. In moments of alarm these hairs stand up stiffly, catching and reflecting the light. Even from far away, other pronghorns see the bouncing cushion flash as the animal runs from danger, and they in turn relay the signal for miles across the sunlit plains.

But though they were wary and on guard, the pronghorns could also be curious. The historian Francis Parkman, who crossed the high plains in the pioneering days of 1846, wrote that "they would approach to look at me, gaze intently with their great round eyes, then suddenly leap aside and stretch lightly away over the

A self-taught artist from New York named William Cary painted the combat of two bull bison from sketches he made on his western trips in the 1860's and '70's. It was by such battles that the leader of the herd maintained his position against the constant challenges of the younger bulls.

In plowing under the tough buffalo grass of the plains, white men so upset the balance of nature that they literally reaped a whirlwind. This grim photograph of a ruined farm was taken in the Dust Bowl in 1937.

prairie, as swiftly as a race-horse."

From Parkman we have some of the most vivid pictures of that wilderness as it once was. "The prairie teemed with life," he wrote. "The face of the country was dotted far and wide with countless hundreds of buffalo. . . . Squalid, ruffian-like wolves sneaked through the hollows and sandy ravines. Several times I passed through villages of prairie dogs, who sat, each at the mouth of his burrow, holding his paws before him in a supplicating attitude, and yelping away most vehemently, whisking his little tail with every squeaking cry he uttered. Prairie dogs are not fastidious in their choice of companions; various long checkered snakes were sunning themselves in the midst of the village, and demure little gray owls, with a large white ring around each eye, were perched side by side with the rightful inhabitants."

Parkman also tells of the weather of the region. "Not a breath of air over the free and open prairie; the clouds were like light piles of cotton; and where the blue sky was visible, it wore a hazy and languid aspect. The sun beat down upon us with a sultry, penetrating heat. At last, towards evening the old familiar black heads of thunder-clouds rose fast above the horizon, and the same deep muttering of distant thunder that had become the ordinary accompaniment of our afternoon's journey began to roll hoarsely over the prairie. Only a few minutes elapsed before the whole sky was densely shrouded. . . . Suddenly from the densest fold of the cloud the flash leaped out, quivering again and again down to the edge of the prairie; and at the same instant came the sharp burst and the long rolling peal of thunder. A cool wind, filled with the smell of rain, just then overtook us, leveling the tall grass by the side of the path."

Storms like this sweep the Great Plains today. The pronghorns are there, still alert and wary, but still curious, coming to the edge of the highway to look at a passing car. The prairie dogs and their co-tenants, rattlesnakes and burrowing owls, may still be seen, though there are far fewer of them now. But the bison are gone. From millions, in a few decades they were reduced to hundreds, and if it had not been for the efforts of a few people to save them, they might have vanished entirely. Today, in several western parks and reservations, herds of them are protected, but as wild animals they are gone forever.

How did it happen? The answer is the same as for the passenger pigeon and the Carolina parakeet; with rifles they were easy to kill, and there were men eager to do the killing. The story is one of wasteful but systematic extermination, of bison carcasses left to rot in hundreds by hunters who took only the hide, or the head for a trophy, or even only the tongue. The coming of the railroads, the ranchers, and the wheatgrowers all had something to do with the decline of the bison, once the most numerous grazing animal on earth.

With each of these developments, some of the short grass on which the bison grazed went, too. Here plowed up to make way for wheatfields, there overgrazed by sheep and cattle, the age-old underground moisture-conserving root system which kept the soil firm has been badly disturbed or destroyed. Floods in wet seasons and dust storms in times of drought are the result, for the weather of the high plains remains, as it always was, violent and unpredictable.

Compared with other parts of the country, the high plains are still open and empty-looking. Though greatly and sadly changed by the coming of white men, they still have the look and feel of wilderness—a perpetual wilderness of space.

73

5

Desert Pageant

Although nineteenth-century mapmakers were mistaken when they called the plains the Great American Desert, explorers soon discovered, between the Rockies to the east and the Sierra Nevada to the west, a true desert.

This arid wilderness extends as far north as Oregon and as far south as Mexico, covering large areas of Nevada, Utah, Arizona, and New Mexico—plus parts of Idaho, Texas, and Wyoming as well. It is a region of little rainfall, of hot days and cold nights, of intense light and shimmering distances and fantastic landscapes. To the men who crossed it, it was more a place of terror than of beauty, and their routes could be followed by their graves.

Desert—to some people the word calls up a picture of mile after mile of huge sand dunes. Yet few places but the White Sands region of New Mexico and Death Valley in California are anything like that. In North America the desert wilderness means many things. In the Great Basin desert of Nevada and Utah, it means hundreds of square miles of sagebrush and creosote bush, with here and there a smooth, dazzling white valley floor,

Francisco Coronado's army marches over the southwestern desert in 1540, searching for the riches of the seven cities of Cibola. The expedition had a peerless record of discovery, yet Spain regarded it a failure.

the salty remnant of a dried-up lake.

Or it can mean the blue waters of Great Salt Lake itself, rimmed by purple mountains which from a distance seem as totally barren as the mountains of the moon. But in fact they are far from what men will one day find on the waterless, airless moon. At closer range, those mountain slopes turn out to be dotted with juniper; concealed in the rocky flanks are deep canyons, where trees grow tall along foaming mountain torrents.

For arid as it is, the desert does have some rainfall, and the tops of the scattered mountain ranges throughout the region get most of it. Some of these ranges, especially those in northern Arizona and New Mexico, are thickly forested with pine, oak, and aspen. Lower down, even in the desert, there are rivers bordered with willows and cottonwoods, much as there are in the Great Plains. On their fertile banks, crops were being raised by Indian tribes long before the coming of white men. But the beds of many other streams are mere stony washes or arroyos, where water flows only after a rain—and in the desert that rain is usually a cloudburst.

In many places the desert is a region of weird, fantastically colored rock formations—buttes, mesas, gorges, arches, pinnacles, and sheer canyon walls banded with red, rose, and tawny yellow. The Painted Desert of northern Arizona is a dreamlike expanse of rock and sand where shifting tones of crimson, pink, and purple drench the landscape as far as the eye can see. There are also the petrified remains of a forest which grew there more than 160 million years ago.

This wilderness of timeless grandeur is also capable of moments of brief, sudden loveliness. After the winter rains, what was bare ground days before—and will be again in a few days more—is a carpet of low-growing multicolored blossoms. The paloverde thickets that line the washes are suddenly a mist of yellow flowers. The thorny stems of the ocotillo become leafy wands tipped with scarlet. Among the spines of desert cacti there appears a silken explosion of white, yellow, orange, and red flowers.

But many of the plants of the sun-baked regions of California, New Mexico, and Arizona have a nightmarish look about them. Ancient black Joshua trees seem to be made of hundreds of angry fists, each flourishing a handful of knives. The creamy-white blossoms of the yucca, or Spanish bayonet, rise from a barricade of swordlike spikes. The cholla, or jumping cactus, wears what looks at a distance like soft, cream-colored fur; it is actually covered with minute, stinging needles.

Towering overhead are huge, ribbed, faceless giants out of a madman's dream, their bodies and enormous handless arms dense with spines. These are the saguaros, strangest of all the desert's menagerie of strange plants. They grow nowhere in the world but in northern Mexico, south-

The dry, cactus-studded landscape of Arizona's Gila River Basin, which has supported an Indian civilization for 9,000 years, is shown at left in a 19th-century sketch by Heinrich Möllhausen. The iguana below was drawn in Mexico in 1789 by a member of a party exploring New Spain. The lizard was highly prized for its meat and eggs by the Indians.

Mountain streams and desert springs support lush pockets of wildlife in the otherwise scorched drylands. This oil painting, recently found in Mexico where it had been gathering dust for more than two centuries, depicts a Spanish hunting party taking its stock of game at an oasis in the southwest.

ern Arizona, and a few spots in California; and even within this narrow range they do not grow everywhere.

But where they do grow, they dominate the landscape. A saguaro forest is one of the most spectacular sights in a land full of spectacles. They grow forty or fifty feet high—some even as high as seventy-five feet—in a region where normally only about ten inches of rain falls in a year. Their secret lies in the way they are able to store up water when it does rain. The deep accordion pleats that furrow their trunks expand as their spreading roots soak up moisture from the ground. A large saguaro may weigh nine or ten tons, and even in the midst of a dry spell, that weight is three-quarters water. But to a thirsty traveler it would be no help; the juice of the saguaro is too bitter to drink.

Unpromising though the spiny, arid wilderness of the saguaros may appear to a wandering human, it is home to a surprising number of animal inhabitants. Doves and thrashers nest even among the terrible spines of the cholla cactus. Woodpeckers and flickers drill nesting holes in the trunks of the saguaros. They drill so many, in fact, that some are left over, becoming shelters for little desert owls and even for snakes and lizards. At night, long-eared desert jack rabbits, foxes, and small, fierce wild pigs, called peccaries or javelinas, roam the cactus regions. In tunneled underground galleries live scores of harmless rodents known as kangaroo rats (though they are hardly bigger than mice). They are unique among all animals in that they are able to live without ever drinking a drop of water.

Other desert dwellers are not so harmless. Scorpions, armored relatives of spiders, come out from under desert stones at night, bearing a deadly sting at the tip of their long, curved tails. There are desert snakes called sidewinders because of their habit of moving over the sand by looping themselves sideways. There are Gila monsters, huge, flabby lizards whose pebbly pink-and-black markings make them almost invisible on the desert floor, and whose bite is highly dangerous.

Other smaller lizards abound in the desert, and they are the main diet of a desert bird known as the road runner, or chaparral cock. The size of a chicken, with long legs and a long tail that jerks up and down with each passing reaction—one can almost see him think—the road runner is a comical sight as he zigzags and scurries across the desert floor in search of something to eat. His wings are too short for expert flying, but they keep him buoyant as he swoops along, clearing boulders, gliding over gullies. In a ravenous mood he will snap up whatever runs or crawls—grasshoppers, spiders, mice, centipedes, scorpions, even a snake.

Into this strange land, early in the year 1540, there rode an army of some three hundred Spaniards. They had come north from Mexico in search of

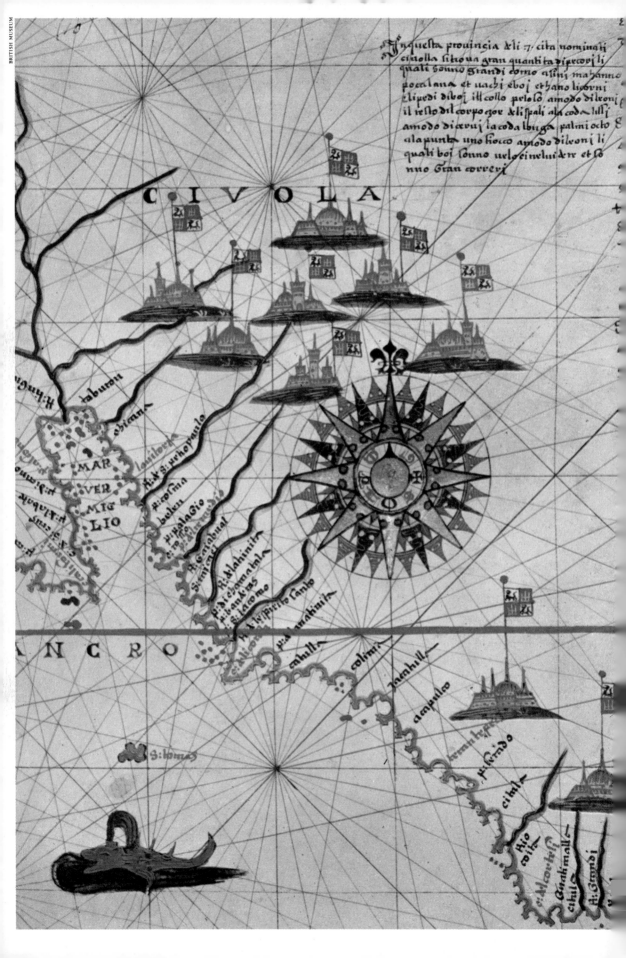

the seven legendary golden cities of Cibola. Never before or since has there been an exploring party quite like this one. Its leader, General Francisco Vásquez de Coronado, was dressed in glittering armor, his helmet adorned with plumes. His chief officers also wore full armor, and others were dressed in chain mail or heavy leather coats. Each day they went deeper through what is now Arizona and New Mexico into the desert wilderness, gaping at its weird shapes, its lurking, scuttling life, its white spaces undulating with heat. The conquistadors were weighted down with crossbows, arquebuses, lances, and swords; their provisions were loaded on hundreds of pack animals, and herds of sheep and cattle trailed along. With them came a thousand Indians.

Behind all this splendor, like some Old World tapestry brought to life in a heathen land, lay one obsession—the hope of finding gold. Rumors of gold had been brought back to Mexico by Cabeza de Vaca who, after three years of wandering, finally found his way back into the regions Cortes had conquered for Spain. De Vaca spoke of vast herds of "hunch backed cows"—the first report of the bison—but the Spaniards were not much interested in animals. They were inter-

The seven cities of Cibola (top) were supposedly built by seven bishops fleeing from the Moorish invasion of Portugal in the 8th century. An Italian cartographer put them near the Gulf of California in his 1578 chart.

ested in what the wanderer had not seen but only heard about: "large and powerful villages four and five stories high," their walls encrusted with gold and jewels.

Coronado found no golden cities, for there were none—only Zuñi pueblos, the greatest of which were poor, dusty places compared to what the Spaniards had expected to see. In his report Coronado admitted ruefully, "The Seven Cities are seven little villages."

Although more vague rumors and the dogged hope of yet finding gold took some of the army all the way into what is now Kansas, they were rewarded with nothing more than an encounter with the herds of "hunch backed cows." They endured trouble with hostile Indian tribes, hunger, thirst, and blazing heat that turned armor into an oven—all for nothing. After three years, what remained of the expedition, broken and defeated, made its way back to Mexico. As far as the Spaniards were concerned, they had discovered nothing at all.

But another party of Coronado's men, dispatched to the northwest in search of water, had made a discovery. Rumors of a great river in that desert region were as eagerly followed up as rumors of gold. Such a rumor, picked up from Indians, led a party commanded by Captain López de Cárdenas to the edge of a precipice. There, at the bottom of an abyss a mile deep, lay a silent silver thread—the water they had come to find. For three days

Some of the desert's vibrant coloring is seen in these delicate cactus blossoms. The species above was named for George Engelmann, a German-born botanist who toured the west in 1835.

they tried to discover a way down the rocky, jagged, cliff-walled canyon. Finally they gave up. The Grand Canyon, one of the wonders of the world, was to its discoverers what it would be to thirsty men after them—a magnificent hell, where needed water rushed tantalizingly out of reach.

From the rim of the Grand Canyon today the same silent silver thread can be traced at the bottom—though in fact it is a raging torrent, over a hundred yards wide and as much as forty-five feet deep. The Colorado River has been following the same course ever since the Rocky Mountains were uplifted millions of years ago. Over the ages the rock has been slowly pushing up and up, lifting the high lookout a dizzy mile up from the river's course. And the river goes on cutting the canyon deeper. That great stream carries every day one-half million tons of sand and silt, torn from the rock along its course, into the Gulf of California.

The Colorado, second largest river in the United States, has its headwaters deep within the Rockies, far above sea level. It drops eight feet to the mile, compared to a drop of four inches to the mile along the mighty Mississippi. This is what makes the Colorado a wild, tumbling river that can cut through solid rock like a buzz saw. It did not need to follow the habit of other rivers, which flow around mountains. It cut straight through, keeping to its course as the earth's crust was lifted around it.

For more than three centuries after

Cárdenas and his men first looked over its rim, the Grand Canyon of the Colorado remained all but totally unexplored. The continent had been crossed repeatedly, but a vast dome of arid land remained an unmapped mystery. This was the Colorado plateau. Rising to a height of 8,000 feet, with stark, stony horizons and no surface streams, it threatened anyone trying to cross it with death from thirst. But it contained a mystery. Two big rivers, the Grand and the Green, came out of the snowfields of the Rockies in Colorado and Wyoming and disappeared into canyons at the northeast edge of the plateau. A thousand miles away, at the southern tip of Nevada, the Colorado River came tumbling out through Boulder Canyon. What happened in between?

In 1869 a one-armed veteran of the Civil War, Major John Wesley Powell, decided to follow the wild, unmapped course of the river across the plateau in the hope of learning the answer. With nine men in four boats, Major Powell entered the canyon at the town of Green River, Wyoming. Three months later, he and five companions emerged into open country in Nevada, where Mormon settlers greeted them.

They had lived through one of the wildest and most dangerous expeditions ever made by explorers of the wilderness. Their story was a terrible one—a tale of treacherous rapids and eddies, repeated capsizings, and almost unendurable temperatures, of spoiled and dwindling food supplies.

Along the way, four frightened members of the party turned back; three were later murdered by Indians.

But through all of this Major Powell's primary concern was with the bands of varicolored rock, layer upon layer, which made up the canyon walls. In those colored bands lay the key to an enormous revelation. They are in fact hardened layers of lava, sand, or sediment which in past ages were the upper surface of land or the bottom of lakes or seas. They contain the remains of animals and plants which lived millions of years ago.

Black rocks at the bottom of the canyon are the roots of mountains, once lofty, which had been worn down into flat plains before there was any life on earth. Read from the bottom upward, the story rushes from age to age like a weird time-lapse movie in which mountains rise and are worn down, and seas come and go. Here is visible evidence of how the earth's surface, which appears so permanent, has been pushed up and down, this way and that, tilted, folded, and cracked, all through its long geological history.

Among those layers are silhouettes in stone of seashells, ferns, and armor-plated fish. On a shelf along the middle of the mile-high wall are footprints of four-footed monsters, unlike any animal now alive, which walked there when the spot was a beach on the shore of an inland sea. The limestone which once lay at the bottom of that sea contains shells, corals, sponges,

A storm breaks dramatically over the gaping pit of the Grand Canyon; a mile below the canyon rim, the mighty Colorado (left center) appears threadlike as it gouges a course ever deeper. Thomas Moran's massive canvas, painted about 1873, once hung in the Capitol at Washington.

and here and there the remains of sharks' teeth.

Even the topmost layer along the canyon wall is many millions of years old. Later layers, which contained the story of more recent and familiar plants and animals, have long ago been worn away. In other parts of the desert wilderness, however, later installments are still to be found. They may be seen in the sculptured rock of Zion Canyon in Utah, where records of the past are stored in 3,000-foot cliffs banded with red and white, at Rainbow Natural Bridge in the expanses of the Painted Desert, and among the fallen trunks of the Petrified Forest.

In certain places the desert seems scarcely changed since white men first saw it four hundred years ago. Some of the pueblos Coronado visited— Acoma and Zuñi in New Mexico— still exist as living villages, and the life of their inhabitants goes on much as it did then. They still grow corn and beans and squashes, make jewelry, baskets, and pots in the same designs, and carry on year after year their vivid ceremonial dances. And all through the region, the vast, open, sun-baked desert land remains as though unalterable.

All the same, there have been changes, some of an awesome kind. History was made in the New Mexican desert on a day in 1945 when the mushroom cloud of the first atomic bomb boiled up from a remote valley. Ghost towns and abandoned mines dot the landscape, and in valleys where once winding groves of cottonwood and willow or thickets of mesquite were the only signs of life there are now sprawling, prosperous cities. Throughout the region are irrigated oases where wheat, alfalfa, cotton, melons, oranges, and dates grow.

Irrigation means a controlled water supply, and this means dams and reservoirs. Few man-made changes anywhere in the wilderness are more spectacular than those brought about by these great structures, which can alter the course of rivers, harness them for power, and create vast lakes where none existed before.

It might seem that with so much water available for irrigation the desert must be shrinking. But the truth is neither so simple nor so happy. As in the Great Plains, misuse and overgrazing in the days of the open range meant that desert moved in. Where grass once grew, the prickly pear and other dry-land plants moved in. Where forests of mesquite were cut for fence posts and fuel, some of the land's ability to hold on to moisture was lost. While irrigation has moistened some corners of the desert, others are becoming drier. The water table—the underground supply of water on which trees like the mesquite and plants like alfalfa depend—is going down.

The white man, for all his ingenuity, has not succeeded in conquering the desert wilderness. That, perhaps, is the chief reason for its strange and awesome fascination.

Strangely gnarled Joshuas (above), called "the most repulsive tree in the vegetable kingdom" by explorer John C. Frémont, surround a caravan crossing the Mojave Desert in 1867. Hoping to simplify desert travel, a group of western mine owners imported twenty camels from Mongolia in the early 1860's, resulting in the bizarre sight below.

6

The Majestic Northwest

The mountain men were known to be the biggest liars in the west. These gaunt, rough trappers, who disappeared behind the Rocky Mountains for months on end, told their tall tales around the campfires at their yearly rendezvous. They tried to out-drink, out-fight, and out-brag each other, and their bears grew meaner, their mountain lions fiercer, and their trail blazing tougher as the rendezvous went on.

They told of giant trees, of boiling mud that spewed high in the air, of rivers containing more fish than water. John Colter came back to St. Louis in 1810 after he had explored the land beyond the mountains alone, with only a thirty-pound pack, a gun, and a long knife. He told wild tales about geysers, and about a huge, bottomless lake deep in the mountains beyond the desert. The stories seemed so far-fetched that he was laughed at, and for years the region he had seen was known as "Colter's Hell."

Twenty years later there was still laughter when Daniel Potts, another mountain man, wrote about "boiling springs . . . of most beautiful fine clay [that] resembles a mush pot and throws its particles to the immense

This peaceful Rocky Mountain scene, entitled simply Night Camp, *was painted about 1850 by James Wilkins of St. Louis. Wilkins based it on sketches made while accompanying a wagon train to California.*

height of from twenty to thirty feet. The clay is white and of a pink [color] and water appears fathomless as it appears to be entirely hollow under neath. There is also a number of places where the pure sulphur is sent forth in abundance. One of our men visited one of those wilst taking his recreation—there at an instant the earth began a tremendious trembling and he with dificulty made his escape when an explosion took place resembling that of thunder. During our stay in that quarter I heard it every day."

Knowing the reputation of mountain men, nobody was taken in by such yarns. It took another twenty years before easterners were convinced of the awesome wonders of the northwest wilderness.

What the mountain men had explored, in their hunt for beaver, were three majestic mountain systems that emerge from Alaska and flare apart in British Columbia, to continue southward in parallel parades. The Coastal Range fronts the Pacific Ocean, and the Cascade Mountains (which become the Sierra Nevada at the California border) run down the center. With the Rocky Mountains to the east, the three ranges cover nearly one-third of the continent. Within them lies a giant wilderness as fantastic as the legends which grew up about it.

Here are forests of the biggest trees that grow on earth—a dark and pathless woodland of huge columns and massive fallen trunks. Here are abysmal gorges through which course thundering rivers swollen with water melted from northern glaciers. One of these gorges, cut by the Salmon River, is 200 miles long and 4,000 feet deep.

Immense, remote valleys and high mountain meadows are the haunts of some of the world's most superb wild animals. The cougar is a fearful wildcat that hurls itself at its prey like a living torpedo. The big wapiti, with its magnificent antlers, is one of the noblest of all wilderness animals. Black bears and grizzlies growl with a low rumble before making a kill with a pat of their forepaws. And two monarchs, the bighorn sheep and the mountain goat, survey their empire from inaccessible snowy heights.

Beautiful and mysterious sockeye salmon spawn in the rushing rivers. After living for three or four years in the depths of the Pacific Ocean, each year millions of sockeyes gather at the river mouths and fight their way upstream against strong currents and rapids, even leaping up over waterfalls. On long rivers, like the Columbia, or the Yukon in Alaska, the fish may travel 1,500 miles or more. Each one returns to the same lake or stream where it was born.

When a female sockeye, filled with eggs and ready to spawn, arrives in her home stream among the mountains, she picks out a quiet place, where the pure, clear water is about two feet deep and the bottom is clean gravel, and lays her eggs. The male swims over the eggs and fertilizes

The forty-niners who trooped by the thousands into California seeking gold were awed by the wilderness they found there. Their canvas cities sprouted like mushrooms along the streams of the Sierra Nevada; a miner named J. Goldsborough Bruff made this drawing of the inside of a tepee-shaped tent in 1849.

When these drawings were published in 1676, Spain's New World empire extended well into what is now the American northwest. The artist's sketches of the animals he saw in that region include (top to bottom) a cougar, a pronghorn, and a porcupine.

them. Sunk safely among the pebbles, they then ripen during the winter months.

When the eggs hatch, the young sockeyes live for about a year, sometimes longer, as fresh-water fish feeding on insects. Finally they allow themselves to be picked up by the swift current and carried downstream. Down they rush, hundreds of miles, perhaps for many days. Their curving bodies pitch over cascades, whirl in rapids, and are flung against rocks. At length the mouth of the river is reached, and the sockeyes vanish under the Pacific rollers. In some mysterious way they now turn into salt-water fish.

The sockeyes are knights in shining armor among fish. They are the cleanest feeders, the liveliest swimmers, the highest jumpers, the bravest warriors among all the finned inhabitants of the fabulous northwest wilderness.

The interior of this wilderness was unknown and unexplored for more than three centuries after Columbus discovered the New World. Even glimpses of it were few and far between.

The first report was that of the 1542 expedition of Juan Rodríguez Cabrillo, who has been called "the Columbus of the Pacific." Cabrillo was a Spanish explorer who sailed north along the Pacific coast from Mexico in a frail little ship about the size of a Chinese junk. The explorers became lost in a fog, evidently off the coast of northern California, where a

Touring the northwest in the 1840's, Canadian Paul Kane painted Chualpay Indians using wicker baskets to capture the swarming salmon that hurdled even waterfalls on their way upriver to spawn. These falls on the Columbia River have disappeared beneath an artificial lake created by Grand Coulee Dam.

stream brought tremendous logs of fallen redwood trees to the ocean. Redwoods are the tallest trees in the world (one standing today is 364 feet high). When they saw these timbers, two or three times as big as any trees they had ever seen before, the superstitious sailors thought that they were close to a land of terrible giants. They lost no time in putting about and heading south again toward Mexico. Their leader, Cabrillo, had died on the voyage. When the survivors made their report to the Spanish authorities, people swore they would never go to that part of the world again.

Two centuries later, in 1743, when Chevalier de La Vérendrye was on the trail to the Rocky Mountains, a lone man was wandering through the northwest wilderness far beyond him.

He was a Yazoo chief whose tribe lived on the Mississippi River near where the city of Natchez is today. The Indian's name was Moneaucht Apé, which means "The Killer of Pain and Fatigue." He could take anything in the way of hardship. He could not write, but when he was very old, he told his story to French Jesuits who wrote it down in the *Jesuit Relations,* the history of the early French missionaries in America.

Apé was able to live entirely on the food and shelter offered by the wilderness, and so he could travel as far as he pleased. He first went north to the Great Lakes and then east to Niagara Falls. After that he headed west, crossed the prairies, and plunged into the northwest wilderness. On the last lap of his trip to the Pacific he spent sixteen days in a canoe going down the Columbia River to reach a tribe of Indians which he had heard lived on the coast of the "Great Water of the West." After visiting with them for two weeks or so, he proceeded southward along the coast until "severe climate and want of game" caused him to turn back. After five years on the trail, he showed up back home among the Yazoos.

No real news of the northwest wilderness came out of Apé's trip. On his amazing journey he was simply visiting other Indian tribes. As an Indian it was not his nature to be astonished by the immense trees or the spectacular mountains and gorges, or to be disturbed by bears and cougars. Mountains and waterfalls, leaping salmon and rainbows, wapitis, bighorns, eagles—the Indian had long since ceased to be amazed by the splendors of the wilderness that was his home.

When Apé saw the coastal waters of the northwest wilderness, they still teemed with carefree sea otters. These comical animals would dive a hundred feet or more to pick up shellfish from the sea bottom, shoot back up to the surface, then float on their backs,

The spectacular redwood forests of the Pacific coast caused early explorers to speak of the region as a land of giants. This painting of an Indian camp in a grove of redwoods is by the American artist Albert Bierstadt.

rocking in the waves, as they feasted
off the shellfish which they had placed
on their stomachs. The sea otter's
beautiful fur, the most valuable in
the world, was a lure to thousands of
otter-catchers in the last half of the
eighteenth century. First came the
Russians, then the Spanish and the
English. After the Revolution, Americans made the long voyage around
Cape Horn to compete for the wealth
of sea otters. This remote area was
wide open to all comers, for most of
it was unknown and unclaimed.

Two of the hardiest trees in the
world grow along this bleak northern
coast. Sitka spruce, with one and a
half inch needles like steel pins, stand
on the most exposed headlands, taking the full force of ocean storms. The
constant winds leave the Sitka spruce
shaped like a torn, violently waving
flag, yet so rigid that it seems to be
as motionless as a tree in a painting.
Where dunes are piled up at the
mouths of ravines, and not even tough
grasses can take hold in the windswept, shifting sand, lodgepole pine
drops its roots to unknown depths for
anchorage and is nourished by the
glistening crystal sand. The silhouette
of this remarkable tree, solitary and
jet black, is etched against the glaring
white sand.

*When a redwood that is many centuries old
falls or is cut down, it is often found to
be hollow. This party, sketched at Mari-
posa, California, in 1873, amuses itself by
riding through such a tunnel-like trunk.*

97

An osprey, a fierce fish hawk, challenges an otter for its salmon catch. This 1844

painting by John James Audubon is one of the naturalist's most impressive works.

Today, as they have through thousands of years, winds off the Pacific collide with snow-capped volcanoes on the Olympic peninsula and unload some 140 inches of rain per year. This is three and a half times the rainfall in woodlands on the eastern side of the continent. The result is a towering rain forest, with a canopy of hemlocks, arborvitaes, and Douglas firs

150 feet and higher above the ground. The floor is heavily cushioned with moss and deep in sword ferns. Huge horizontal branches high above are aerial fern gardens. Giant vines festoon the tall trees, and shafts of sunlight slant down through the mist.

Farther south, beginning at the border of Oregon and California, the famous coastal redwood forests, with

some trees more than three hundred feet tall, are nourished by fogs. Here there are no snow-capped mountains near the coast to cause heavy downpours, but fogs settle in the valleys of the Coastal Range almost every night. The steady dripping of moisture down through the tall forest increases water delivery to the tremendous roots by two or three times an equal amount of

William H. Meyers, a gunner on an American warship, sketched this scene in his journal in 1845. Meyers and several fellow sailors went hunting during a stopover in California, foolishly killed a grizzly-bear cub, and found themselves facing the enraged she-bear.

The wapiti, the largest American deer, still bears the name given it by Shawnee Indians centuries ago. The early English settlers, however, called the beast an elk, which was the name of the European moose familiar to them. William Jacob Hays painted this antlered wapiti and his harem about 1865.

rainfall. There is no tangle of underbrush. The floor of the redwood forest is carpeted by a thick matting of needles, with here and there scatter rugs of bright green sorrel in sunny spots. It is truly a forest cathedral, filled with twilight even at high noon, where the hush is seldom broken by wild animals or birds.

Some rain-bearing clouds off the Pacific override the Coastal Range to deposit heavy snow on the heights of the inland mountains. The Cascades are well watered, and the streams are lined with green trees. Like many wonders in the northwest wilderness, these trees are unique. The alders, instead of being twiggy bushes in swampy places, as they are in the eastern wildernesses, are trees perhaps one hundred feet tall with trunks three feet thick. Their wood is satiny white when freshly cut, but it promptly turns a rich red. Big leaf maple has leaves up to ten inches across. Its trunk, instead of growing vertically, curves out horizontally with a wide arch holding the huge leaves like parasols over small cascara trees, found nowhere else in the world. When white men came, they made medicine out of the bark of the cascara tree. Today, apple and peach orchards bloom in this enclave of the northwest wilderness.

Waterways in the northwestern forests are dotted with stout dams built by beaver to protect their offshore lodges. These well-engineered dams sometimes reach gigantic proportions

—in the Rockies one was found that stretched more than 2,000 feet across the water. The foundations and supports of the dams are made of large trees which the beaver fells upstream and floats down to the work site. Trees near the water are used first, but when they are gone, the beaver may even dig a canal, as much as five hundred feet long, to transport the timber standing farther back.

After a tall tree has been toppled, it is cut into portable lengths for towing. A beaver, swimming alongside, takes a firm grasp on the log with his teeth and, using his flat tail vertically like a rudder, steers it to the spot where it will be used. The dam is then packed with mud, stones, and debris to make it secure.

A beaver lodge, also made with sticks and mud, is built so sturdily that it is occasionally shared by other amphibious animals. Muskrats are likely to stock the cellar with waterlily roots, which the beaver also enjoys. The mink is another winter visitor, using the lodge's submarine exit for excursions under the ice in his hunt for fish. Apparently, the beaver and his guests get along well enough; or if they do not, it is one of the best-kept secrets in the wilderness.

With two mountain ranges extracting the moisture from the Pacific rain clouds, the country between the Sierra Nevada and the Rockies is left a raw, weird desert. Men who came through the Rockies in the early 1800's were amazed to find this desert. They

Cougars—also called panthers, pumas, or mountain lions—were once worshipped as gods by several southern California Indian tribes, which scavenged much of their meat from the carcasses of deer killed by the big cats. This drawing of a cougar was done on a Spanish expedition to California in 1789.

had seen glaciers, roaring mountain streams, deep forests, and many wild animals—then abruptly all of this came to an end. They stared down from the last mountain height at a hot, yellowish, almost lifeless land. They had reached the brink of a vast depression in the northwest mountains that would be called the Great Basin. It includes the High Desert of Oregon, the arid valleys around Great Salt Lake, much of Nevada, and extends southward to include Death Valley.

Before roads were built across the Great Basin, men who tried to cross it suffered terribly. The sharp edges of broken lava gravel cut the feet of horses. Lakes were heavily salted, with no outlets. There were few springs. Rivers, started by cloudbursts in the mountains, sank and vanished. No edible plants or animals were to be seen. Days were fiery, nights bitterly cold.

Jedediah Smith, the hunter and explorer who opened Wyoming's South Pass through which settlers and forty-niners would pour on the Oregon Trail, was the first white man to conquer the Sierra Nevada range, in 1827, and the first to cross the Great Basin. In his journal he put down his impressions of this wasteland: "Ascending a high point of a hill I could discover nothing but sandy plains or dry Rocky hills. . . . With our best exertion we pushed forward, walking as we had been for a long time over the soft sand . . . worn down with hunger and fatigue and burning with thirst increased by the blazing sands. . . . My dreams were not of Gold or ambitious honors but of my distant quiet home, of murmuring brooks of Cooling Cascades." Before he reached safety, Smith told of burying one of the men of his party up to his neck in the sand to conserve what was left of his body moisture while he went on ahead and found life-saving water.

Two amazing plants live vigorously here by distilling whispers of moisture out of the cold night air. Western junipers are widely scattered in some areas of this desert, looking from a distance like black explosions. Somehow this small tree creates hundreds of thousands of tiny leaves in this parched land. Each one has a sparkling, yellow droplet of nonevaporating resin that seals in a speck of moisture, keeping it from being snatched away by the hot sunlight. The bright droplets are very fragrant, perfuming the air for miles around.

The other plant, which peppers many hundreds of square miles of the Great Basin, is the famous sagebrush of the northwest desert, with brittle twigs and dry leaves that rattle in the wind. Sagebrush is scattered and low and offers little shade. Horses shun it for browsing except as starvation rations. It is good only for a campfire, to warm a man who sleeps in the dangerous desert.

How different are the wonders of the surrounding mountains. Massive pine, spruce, and fir forests darken the high slopes of the Rockies. In

Natural wonders of the Yellowstone region, like the boiling, sulphurous spring painted here by Thomas Moran, provided the early mountain men with ammunition for their tall tales. Trapper Jim Bridger swore that in a nearby petrified forest he came across petrified birds singing petrified songs.

the Cascades, Douglas firs, hundreds of years old, go straight up more than two hundred feet, with trunks ten feet thick. Yet they stand so close together in such tight forests that they look like wheatfields when seen from far away. Engelmann spruce forms its slender forests on the moist, cool north sides of the mountains. The seeds of this spruce look like pink tissue paper, but it is a tough, hardy tree.

Other trees have left an astonishing record of their toughness. Excavations into the high cliffs of Specimen Ridge in Yellowstone Park have uncovered the stone fossils of twenty-seven forests, one on top of another. The bottom one was growing in that place some 55 million years ago, when it was buried by volcanic lava. In the course of time another forest grew above the buried stumps of the older one—and this, in turn, was buried by another eruption. And so it went, through millions of years.

In the midst of the forests of the Cascades, Crater Lake marks the site of a tremendous explosion that took place a few thousand years ago. Mt. Mazama, which stood where Crater Lake is today, was one of the highest snow-capped volcanic peaks in the Cascades. After gushing fiery lava for a time, the volcano erupted so violently that nearly five cubic miles of rock and gray pumice dust buried the surrounding wilderness. The Indians who lived in the area were terrified, but this was a small matter compared to what happened next. Sud-denly, the top half of the whole volcano vanished, collapsing into its own crater. During the centuries that followed, the awful hole gradually filled with water until it became the magnificent lake of today. It is the deepest lake in the United States, a rich metallic blue in color, surrounded by yellow cliffs.

But the northwest wilderness holds nothing more spectacular than the wonders the mountain men saw in the Yellowstone region: over one hundred geysers in eight geyser basins; 3,000 springs of boiling water pouring down over terraces of bright-colored rocks; pools of hot mud slowly popping with dome-shaped bubbles; a whole mountain made of volcanic glass, called obsidian, which Indians chipped off to make their arrow points. The Yellowstone River plunges with a great roar over a precipice 308 feet high—nearly twice the height of Niagara. It has carved a canyon a thousand feet deep through solid rock. The colors of the sides of the canyon run from lemon yellow to deep orange, from silver white to black, and its minerals show every tint and tone of red, pink, and brown. This canyon, sculptured and colored by the ages, was the homeland of many wild animals—bighorns and mountain goats, bears, cougars, beaver, black-tailed deer, wapitis.

The mountain men had told the truth—nobody could make up this unearthly corner of the American wilderness.

7

"Seward's Folly"

Alaska, the huge northwestern projection of the continent and the source of the three western mountain chains, contains the greatest wilderness left in America. New York had been a thriving city for a century before Alaska's shores were seen by white men. Until 1867 only its coastline was known. The interior was a blank. That was the year that Secretary of State William Seward bought this northern wilderness from Russia for less than two cents an acre. The transaction was immediately dubbed "Seward's Folly."

The state of Alaska, twice as large as Texas, is a dominion of forests, mountains, glaciers, and tundra, part of it trackless and unexplored. Man can soar over it, as the birds have always done, but his cities, sawmills, mines, fisheries, and oil rigs cling to its coasts and rivers, leaving the bulk of the inland wilderness untouched. There, great American birds and animals lead primeval lives hardly changed since the Ice Age. The bald eagle soars over undisturbed valleys, his eagle eye out for marmots and ptarmigan. The Kodiak bear, towering twelve feet when he walks upright like a man, fishes in streams that are

Vitus Bering died on a desolate island in the Aleutians in December, 1741, soon after making the first sighting of Alaska. His discovery brought Russian fur traders to the fringes of this mighty wilderness.

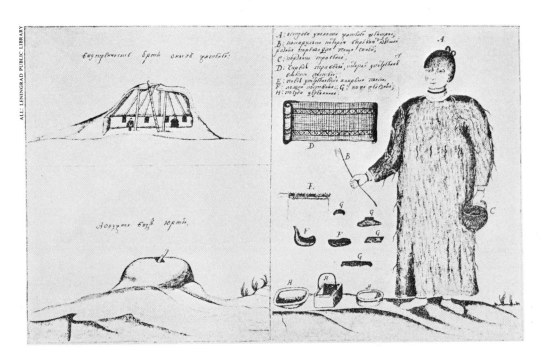

Above is an Aleut woman with the household utensils she used in the earth-covered hut at left, shown from outside and in cross section. Below are the tools and weapons of an Aleut man, who holds a spear and throwing stick.

silver with salmon. Herds of caribou wander across vast lichen pastures.

The discoverer of Alaska found it very dismal and did not even set foot on its shore. In the late summer of 1741, the eighty-foot sloop *St. Peter,* from Siberia, cast anchor in the lee of Kayak Island. Heavy-set, sixty-year-old Vitus Bering stared from her deck at a glistening white peak which appeared and disappeared among storm clouds above a vast black forest. This spectacular view appeared suddenly to Bering and his crew, who had been blinded by fog for weeks while sailing eastward parallel to the Aleutian Islands and the Alaska Peninsula. Without knowing what the land was, Bering named that superb peak Mt. St. Elias, the name it still bears. Then he ordered a landing party to fetch water from the island, returned to his cabin, and went to sleep.

No effort was made to reach the mainland. Among the crew that landed on Kayak Island was a young German botanist named George Steller, who alone seems to have felt the thrill of great adventure. Later, Steller told how he had reveled among discoveries no civilized men had ever gazed upon. He also told of his anguish when sulky, sick old Vitus Bering ordered the landing party to return to the ship after a day ashore. They weighed anchor and set a course westward toward Siberia, racing against the coming winter.

But it was too late. After only about five hundred miles, tortured by savage

These sketches show the hide-covered, kayak-like craft, called bidarkas, in which the Alaskan Indians hunted seals and sea otters. The Russians then paid for the valuable skins with cheap trinkets. The drawing above was made in 1744 by a member of the Bering party; the remaining three pictures on these pages were done by a Russian artist in 1767.

In 1791 a Spanish scientific expedition under Alejandro Malaspina landed at what is now Yakutat Bay on Alaska's southern coast. They called the bay Desengaño (Spanish for disappointment) for it did not lead them to the Northwest Passage they sought.

storms, they had to seek shelter in the lee of an island. But the increasingly violent gale tore the *St. Peter*'s anchors loose, and a great wave lifted the sloop high and smashed her down on the jagged rocks.

It is due to the intelligent Steller, who kept notes, that we know of the bizarre events of this discovery of the Alaskan wilderness. Vitus Bering died on December 8, 1741, and the rest of the party spent the winter hunting and fishing, collecting sea-otter skins, and looking forward fervently to that day in the spring when they could rebuild their vessel and be on their way.

Early in April, when the days were lengthening and the weather becoming warmer, the surviving officers and crewmen started collecting the pieces of the battered wreck and bringing them together at one spot. Four months later they sailed away in a crude ship which they had built. It was forty-one feet long, only half the size of the *St. Peter.* This handmade, "half-pint" vessel was seaworthy enough to carry forty-six men back to Kamchatka, Siberia, where they were received with great excitement—but not because they were safe nor because they had seen Alaska. Nobody cared what they had seen.

The Malaspina expedition saw the Alaskan Indian burial ground at top; the tall platforms are funeral pyres for cremation. The party also landed at Vancouver Island (center). Returning home, the Spanish vessel encountered ice off South America (bottom).

They brought back with them sea-otter skins, the most costly, most exquisite fur in the world. A man could get a hundred rubles apiece for those skins by trading with the rich Chinese. And the survivors of the Bering expedition said that the waters they had visited teemed with sea otters. This discovery put the Russians on the coast of Alaska for 126 years. In all that time they never spread inland. They only wanted the furs of the beautiful land animals that lived in the sea.

When Secretary Seward paid the two-cents-an-acre price for Alaska, he was buying seacoast. To the Americans, as well as to the Russians, the interior wilderness was worthless. Few people went inland until almost 1900— it was too far, too cold, and the mountains were too high. The spring crackup came suddenly in a day, sending murderous blocks of ice hurtling along wilderness streams. This was the signal for swarms of black flies and mosquitoes to rise out of the tundras and blow through the interior wilderness like soot. Only Eskimos and Indians, who were as native to the land as the caribou and bears, could find their way through the never-ending forests.

Then, in 1896, gold was discovered a thousand miles up the Yukon River, and men had to get there or die trying. They pushed against the Yukon's current for weeks and weeks in frail canoes and little steamers, or trekked a few miles a day with dog teams over high mountain passes. Soon afterward, attention shifted to the Seward Peninsula. This is a huge, blunt thumb of land 180 miles long and 130 miles wide, thrusting west toward Siberia. Its tip is washed by the Bering Strait, where only fifty-six miles of water separate the United States and Russia. It is a savage country of naked rock, bare hillsides, and barren valleys, with scarcely a clump of spruce or a salmon stream. It is almost uninhabited and indeed unfit for habitation. Men crossing the peninsula with their dog teams grew to hate the unceasing wind. It took on a personal, brutal character, seeming to inflict the utmost torture possible. Indians called it "the wind beast."

Lying between the Bering Sea and the Arctic Ocean, the Seward Peninsula is remote from the outside world. Fearless navigators in small, sturdy sailing vessels had occasionally ventured into the region. For the most part these waters were uncharted, dim gray expanses which dissolved into vague fog in summer; in the winter there was no horizon line, and the ice appeared to be continuous with the sky. Ever since the sea covered the Bering land bridge from Asia, it is impossible to think of any people living on the Seward Peninsula, except for one reason—"pay dirt."

The sands on the beaches and in nearby creeks sparkled with gold. Thus, by 1899, the city of Nome had sprung up on the Bering shore where there was no harbor, no roadstead, no shelter or protection of any kind.

Here were streets and rows of houses, with a department store where clocks, rugs, and curtains were sold. Here was a jeweler's shop with gleaming displays of gold ornaments and carved fossil ivory.

Nome was isolated for eight months of the year. Its only communication with the outside world took place when navigation was open on the Bering Sea from June to October. Freight was delivered from Seattle, a twelve-day steamship voyage away. Smaller craft carrying travelers and traders had a particularly hard time because of the dangerous, roundabout passage through the foggy Aleutian Islands. To avoid this, people took a short cut, the Katmai Trail, across the base of the Alaska Peninsula, making it from the shore beside Mt. Katmai to the coast of the Bering Sea in three or four days. When the Nome bonanza was at its height, this was a major travel route for Eskimos, Indians, sourdoughs and adventurers.

The Katmai Trail, and the appalling thing that happened to it, illustrates the isolation, terror, and splendor of the Alaskan wilderness.

Early in June, 1912, a mysterious rumble was heard along the trail. This was followed by an uncanny swaying of bushes and the bouncing and trembling of rocks where the trail climbed the valley beside Mt. Katmai to go over the pass. These weird disturbances continued for some ninety hours when suddenly Mt. Katmai blew up with a gigantic roar,

The towering, snow-capped volcanic peaks of Trinity Island off the Alaska Peninsula were seen by many explorers. By 1778 the island was occupied by Russian fur traders who staunchly claimed the land for the czar.

sending a fountain of ash and pumice a thousand feet into the air. At the same time, huge cracks opened at Katmai Pass, and out poured an avalanche of red-hot sand and fiery gases.

When it was all over, seven cubic miles of sand, rock, and pumice had been coughed up, burying the valley of the Katmai Trail, four miles wide and seventeen miles long, to a depth of seven hundred feet. Nobody ever saw the trail again. Instead, a crust formed on the fiery avalanche, perforated by thousands of vents through which imprisoned steam continued to pour.

Today, a half-century later, this eerie, terrifying wasteland is still cooling off, the tremendous internal pressures gradually subsiding. Yet, in every direction across the valley, steam and gases still pour out from countless fissures. This new-born wilderness is called the Valley of Ten Thousand Smokes.

A few miles away, on the western slope of Mt. Katmai, there are a number of peculiar glaciers. Glaciers usually move slowly down valleys, and they must be fed constantly by mountain snow fields above them. These glaciers lost their parent snow fields, yet they do not shrink. They have stood immobile, the same size, for fifty years, thanks to a five-foot coating of volcanic ash insulating them from sun and rain.

There is another oddity in this region—rocks that blow in the wind.

117

Sourdoughs reported that the winds in Katmai Pass were so strong that they picked up sizable rocks and blew them across the ground and even through the air. Outsiders enjoyed such stories, just as easterners once laughed at the tales of the mountain men. Scientists now know that such boulders are light, porous volcanic rock, or pumice, made of the crusts of volcanic bubbles.

Offshore from Katmai, Kodiak Island is the home of the largest carnivore on earth—the Kodiak bear, a giant edition of the grizzly. Because he fears nothing, this calm, plodding monarch seldom gets excited. He is so strong that he can kill a bull moose with a slap, and then carry off the body—although it may weigh half a ton.

The Kodiak bear, unlike the black bear, does not amble around. He knows where he wants to go and makes a direct path to that spot. The straight line of his trail can be seen from afar, across tundra moss and up steep slopes where a man would climb by winding back and forth. The Kodiak has huge spreading paws; one footprint, found in a dried-up mudhole where its outline was clear, covered sixty-nine square inches. On such padded snowshoes, the big bear can tread with ease in deep snow, or on boggy ground and ice.

Despite his ponderous bulk and usually slow, deliberate movements, a Kodiak bear is so agile with his front paws that he can slap vigorous salmon right out of the water. A man is seldom quick enough to do this. In May, when the salmon appear from the sea and start upstream to

118

The slaughter of the animal inhabitants of Alaska's coastal waters began early and was pursued ruthlessly. At left is an 1815 sketch of Aleut children killing young sea lions. The cruel scene above of sealers at work was photographed in 1897. The water color of the grumpy-looking walrus below was painted by a member of Captain Cook's crew.

Dreams of a Northwest Passage lured adventurers from all over the world to the rocky coast of Alaska. There, in 1786, a party of French explorers drowned in a shipwreck, a disaster memorialized twenty years later in this painting by Louis-Philippe Crepin.

All kinds of four-legged beasts were used in the Klondike gold rush. Angora goats pulled photographer E.A. Hegg's darkroom and supply sleds.

spawn, the bear stands on a sandbar in about two feet of water, waiting patiently. When a silvery fish flashes by his legs, down into the water darts a paw. Soon the bear strides contentedly over to the bank of the stream with a thrashing two-foot salmon secured between his jaws.

Nearly a thousand miles straight north from Kodiak Island, deep in the interior of Alaska, is the amazing tundra empire. This is an endless expanse of ponds and muskeg bogs, lichen-covered rocks, clumps of crowberry and blueberry, dwarf willow and birch, that goes on and on over the horizon. Beneath this quilt of life

the ground is permanently frozen so that water cannot soak in. Thus, the surface of the ground is as moist as a rain forest. Under the influence of the long days and the bright northern lights of summertime, ankle-deep carpets of arctic flowers fairly explode among the moss and lichens.

This is the breeding place of millions of birds that come from all over the world. The Arctic tern flies here halfway around the globe from Antarctica. Old squaw ducks and red-throated loons cross a hemisphere to a pin point in this gigantic land, returning to the same nests which they left the year before. The snowy owl,

122

The goal of Klondike prospectors was rough-and-ready Dawson, in Canada near the Alaskan border. Hegg photographed its main street in 1898.

Arctic hare, and blue fox come out of their winter shelters in the taiga, the thin forest of spruce, larch, and fir fringing the tundra. Lemmings, thousands of them, live on the tundra the entire year. In winter, when the thermometer stands at 50 degrees below zero and the tundra is a desert of swirling snow, the small, mouselike lemmings are very comfortable in their homes under the snow, among the roots of the bushes.

The musk ox lives out in the open on the tundra the year round. This antique beast was left there in the Ice Age, and he is still there. In the winter he wears a heavy wool coat that hangs down like an unkempt curtain, protecting his belly from the wind. He feeds on the enormous crops of cotton grass, blueberry, birch, alder, and willow which spring up from the tundra in summer. Like caribou and reindeer, musk oxen live on lichens in the wintertime, browsing among acres of this marvelous plant that have been cleared of snow by the wind.

Even so, how has such an animal survived on the tundra for 20,000 years when his Ice Age companions, the mammoth and the woolly rhinoceros, have perished? For one thing, the mammoth and rhinoceros were

A large segment of the human swarm that descended on the Klondike gold fields was funneled through Chilkoot Pass in Alaska's coastal mountains. In this photograph, a seemingly endless line of prospectors climbs the last thousand feet to the summit of the pass. It sometimes took a man six hours to scale the steep, slick wall of ice.

Caribou (above) still roam the Arctic tundra of Alaska and Canada. Another tundra dweller is the hardy musk ox (right). Its hair is the longest of any North American animal, often growing to a length of three feet. Once on the verge of extinction, herds of musk oxen are now being re-established in northern Alaska.

much larger, probably too large to live for eight months on lichens alone. The musk ox is about the size of a small horse.

Moreover, musk oxen have a form of defense like nothing else in the animal kingdom. They can fend off the most vicious attacks of wolves and bears by bunching together, with the bull members of the herd standing shoulder-to-shoulder and facing outward in what military men call a hollow square. The cows and calves take their places in the center, although some of the calves might hide behind the curtains under the bellies of the bulls. Should a ravenous wolf get too close, the nearest musk ox flashes out of the square like a thunderbolt, puts down his head, hooks the wolf on his horns, and tosses the body away. Then the musk ox, without turning around, backs up and takes his place in the formation, looking as though nothing had happened.

The musk oxen that survived the Ice Age and were so well able to hold off their natural enemies should have enjoyed unique security in their Arctic pastures. But the animals attracted into their sanctuary a new kind of enemy. Eskimos found their meat more delicious than whale and caribou. The deep, oily musk-ox blubber was their best fuel, and the hard bone of musk-ox horns made bows, spearheads, knives, and many tools. When the day came that Eskimos and Indians went after the musk oxen with high-powered rifles, the ancient hollow square was no longer a defense.

Then white men intervened on the side of the musk oxen, which were on the verge of extermination. It was made unlawful to kill the animals, and 15,000 square miles of the best lichen pastures were set aside for them. The few remaining herds were moved into this area, where they have been breeding. Today some 13,000 musk oxen are living in the Arctic tundra—most of them in Canada, a few in Alaska—in conditions much the same as in the Ice Age.

The age-old wilderness is more intact in Alaska than in any other sizable region of the country. The Tongass National Forest covers four hundred miles of islands off Alaska's lower coast, containing 16 million acres of one of the world's finest forests. Bulldozers, with sawmills in their wake, are attacking its flanks with more intensity every year. In the interior, 133 million acres of forest land are almost untouched; about a million acres are devastated by fire every year. Offshore in the Bering Sea an ancient herd of giant fur seals breeds unmolested on a fog-shrouded island. Bighorn sheep still roam among the glaciers and peaks near Mt. McKinley, the highest mountain on the continent. Below them in the forests are the haunts of grizzlies, deep enough so that many survive even though the profound stillness of the last true American wilderness is often rent by the crack of rifles.

127

Pacific Paradise

Probably the darkest, deadest place on the surface of the earth is at the bottom of the Pacific Ocean, under three miles of water. At that spot, some twenty million years ago, the heavy black rock which is the inner crust of the earth suddenly split. A huge scar in the bowl of the Pacific appeared, forming a trench thirty miles wide in some places and over 10,000 feet deeper than the ocean floor. Along the entire length of this crack occurred terrific volcanic eruptions, with raging fires and boiling lava.

The colossal crack did not tap just one pocket of gas and melted rock as in most volcanic explosions, when the underground pressure is soon relieved and the eruption dies down; it must have tapped an immense system of pockets in the earth's crust. The volcanoes continued to gush fire, ashes, and lava for millions of years. Thus, along the 2,000-mile crack, volcanic mountains rose higher and higher until their tops thrust above the sea into the air and sunshine.

It is estimated that this chain of peaks appeared above the water about five million years ago. The highest of them, Mauna Kea, reaches 33,476

In 1778 Captain James Cook stumbled on the Hawaiian Islands while sailing eastward across the Pacific to search for a water route through North America. This print shows Cook's men rowing ashore at Kauai.

feet from the ocean floor, making it the highest mountain on earth, higher even than Mt. Everest. Today, these mountaintops are known as the Hawaiian Islands, the newest state in the Union.

The vast turmoil in the earth's crust at the bottom of the Pacific, begun so many millions of years ago, still continues. The volcanic mountain of Mauna Loa is still pouring out fresh layers of lava. The rim of its crater has lifted more than two miles above the sea, its flanks sloping three miles down into the dark depths of the mid-Pacific. Another volcano is building up just south of Mauna Loa. It is on the way to adding another island to the Hawaiian chain. No one can tell how fast it is rising, or when fresh new acreage—at first a barren and sizzling wilderness—will be added to our fiftieth state.

At the other end of the Hawaiian chain is the island of Kure, 1,400 miles northwest of Honolulu. Its fires died down so long ago that its top has been removed by the erosion of wind and rain. This weird crumb of volcanic wilderness, the westernmost spot in the United States, exists only because coral animals built a collar of reef in the water around the base of the volcano. These tiny animals cannot live deep in the ocean. To survive they must have the warm sunlight that filters through the shallow surf. As the dead volcano sank, the coral animals built their structure higher and higher. Today the original volcano

cone is out of sight beneath the water.

Over the ages, great storms hurled mountainous waves at the reef, pulverizing its upper parts so that tides and currents built a low and irregular island of coral sand within the reef. This sand dune island, less than one-half square mile in area, is surrounded by a great coral ring fifteen miles in circumference.

The Kure atoll, which rises through water so deep that it cannot be estimated by a ship's sounding line, has been the scene of tragic shipwrecks. But undisturbed nature, which quietly creates its varieties of living wildernesses, each in perfect balance, has made it a paradise of birds.

Here is one of the most lively and primeval parts of the American wilderness. During those thousands of years when the dead volcano peak was sinking under the sea, a great crowd of creatures appeared out of the ocean vastness to live on and around the reef built by the coral animals. Few places on the face of the earth teem with such a vigorous and healthy animal population, swaying with the tides, in equilibrium with sea and sky.

The prosperity of an atoll wilderness is due primarily to the constant supply of water, oxygen, and microscopic food delivered fresh every minute by restless currents and breaking waves. As the volcano in the middle of the atoll sank, leaving a lagoon, the coral animals did not permit this to be cut off from the sea. In some

A landscape painted sixty-two years after Cook's discovery depicts the raw beauty of the volcanic plateau of Kauai. The artist is Titian Peale, who had been on Major Long's 1819–20 expedition to the Rocky Mountains and was now exploring the Pacific with Lieutenant Charles Wilkes of the U.S. Navy.

*The Hawaiian volcanoes fascinated Peale. The color notes on his sketch
of Kilauea Pele's western crater were to guide him in a later painting.
Peale also did the painting on pages 134–135 and the one on page 145.*

mysterious way they had the wisdom to leave openings in their reef so that the tides can go in and out.

Thus the lagoon became a tidal aquarium, filled with countless sea urchins and starfish, sea worms and colonies of multicolored sponges. Beautiful bright tropical shellfish are scattered across the floor of the lagoon like jewelry of the sea. In the water above, bell-shaped jellyfish slowly open and close their umbrellas, while oddly-shaped, rainbow-tinted fish dart among them. Families of funny little seahorses live here. Mo-

rays, the largest and most dangerous eels in the world, lurk in caves in the coral reef.

In the course of time a seed arrived on the sandy island and took root. It came from South Pacific islands 2,000 miles away, perhaps carried in the crop of a sea bird. Thus a green place appeared in the middle of the Pacific. A dense, almost impenetrable jungle of scaevola seized the sand pile at Kure. Scaevola is a tough shrub about six feet high, a mass of crooked branches with big, shiny, leathery leaves, loaded with berries like white marbles. This is a fighting shrub with such a strong hold in the sand, and such tough fiber, that it merely flutters in a hurricane.

Countless ghost crabs live in the sand around the scaevola jungle. Turtles lumber up out of the lagoon and lay their eggs here. Birds are everywhere—not gulls, which are creatures of continental shores, but true mid-ocean birds. The lagoon is like a teeming stewpot which, over the course of centuries, lured birds from faraway South Pacific islands.

Here is found the beautiful and astonishing tropic bird, resembling a pinkish-white powder puff from which a comical little face and red beak peek out. The tropic bird has such short legs that it cannot walk; it must fly by rising straight up like a helicopter. Fairy terns build their nests in the fortress of the scaevola bushes. Here the baby terns wait, invisible and safe, while their mother catches live fish for them in the lagoon. She stuffs the wriggling fish down the mouths of her offspring, which swallow them whole despite the fact that the body of the fish is as long as the body of the little fairy tern.

Squadrons of man o'war birds cruise over the tiny atoll. They are the swiftest and lightest birds of the sea. Strangely enough, they cannot light on the sea itself, for they perish at the touch of salt water. The man o'war bird is a ravenous eater. Skillfully adjusting his wings to the wind, he can remain motionless 1,000 feet in the air, waiting to attack other birds rising from the sea with crops full of fish. When a man o'war sees a young tern standing lazily in the sunlight on the sand, he swoops down without touching the ground, snatches the bird, and zooms up. Then, tossing the little tern in the air, the man o'war catches and swallows it in one gulp.

But of all the birds in that island wilderness, the albatross is the most superb and lordly. He glides with scarcely a beat of his long, slender, ten-foot wings, sailing inches above the breaking waves. Albatrosses seek no shelter, but are birds of the windswept beaches, establishing their colonies in the full force of mid-Pacific gales.

The albatross, christened the gooney bird by navy men, seems to be able to fly directly against a strong wind merely by using three or four short wing strokes to gain a certain position in the air. By adjusting the angle of his wings so as to slant like a sloop close-hauled on a windward tack, the albatross soars into the wind with almost no wing beating. It is a perfectly balanced flying machine that can hold a course in highly turbulent air, even low among wave crests, with every feather under split-second control.

OVERLEAF: *As if witnessing a scene in Dante's* Inferno, *members of the Wilkes party gaze spellbound at the boiling caldron of Kilauea. In 1790 the volcano had erupted so violently that it nearly wiped out an army of Hawaiians marching past it to battle.*

AMERICAN MUSEUM OF NATURAL HISTORY

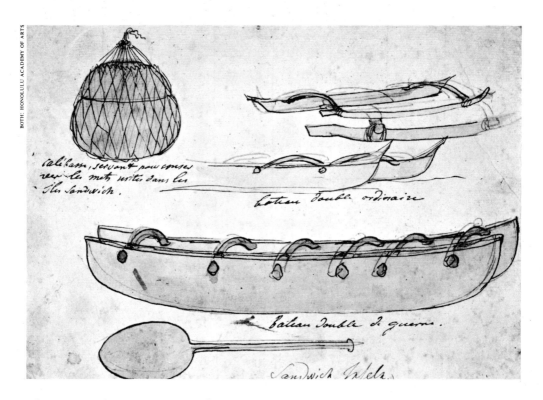

The natives of Hawaii were craftsmen of considerable skill; from the rich variety of woods in the islands they fashioned the food jar and canoes sketched above. The double canoe (bottom) was for military use.

Louis Choris, a young Russian on a round-the-world voyage in 1816, paused at Hawaii and painted the water colors on these and the following two pages. The warriors at right are performing for the royal court.

Mark Twain called Hawaii "the loveliest fleet of islands that lies anchored in any ocean." They are, as well, the most fabulous volcanic wilderness on the face of the globe. Without the three-mile depth of ocean in which they stand, this string of islands would be the most towering mountain range on earth—in a nearly straight, 2,000-mile row are thirty-seven peaks rising 18,000 feet or more from the ocean floor. Since this range was not uplifted by the tilting, bending, and folding of crustal rocks, like granite and sandstone, that formed most of the continental mountain ranges, its composition is quite different. It is built of heavy volcanic basalt rock from the basement of the earth's crust, layers of ash and pumice, and flows of lava piled one on top of another.

This unique wilderness has three zones. The westernmost is the atoll zone—the paradise of birds. This is the oldest of the three, where the volcanoes have died and their peaks have worn down and foundered in the sea. These atolls are visible only because of the coral crowns on them. The middle zone also has long-dead

volcanoes, but they erupted so much later than the atoll zone that remnants of their peaks can still be seen, their slender pinnacles high, tiny islands with steep cliffs.

For example, the island named Gardner Pinnacles is the leftover pieces of the rim of a great crater. It lies 688 miles northwest of Honolulu, its inaccessible rocks rising 190 feet above the sea. This piece of American wilderness totals only about three acres. Nihoa is another crumb of a huge volcanic peak that towers 900 feet, with only one-quarter square mile of dry land. This lonely splinter of a bygone volcano is a magnet for life snatched out of the winds and the sea. Its ridges are grassy, its little valleys have clumps of bushes, and twenty kinds of flowering plants have been counted there. Among these bushes are the nests of legions of small birds, over which the man o'war birds hover. Sea birds lay their eggs along the ledges, and the ocean tides deliver endless supplies of finny fish and shellfish at the foot of the cliffs. Nihoa, like the other steep rock islands of the middle zone, is a com-

plete volcanic wilderness in miniature —self-sustaining, teeming with lusty primeval life.

The third zone, farthest to the southeast, rose up out of the sea much later than the others. It is the beautiful climax of a volcanic wilderness. Its volcanoes are still shooting off their geysers of cinders and spreading their lava. The eight islands of this group have 99 per cent of the dry land of Hawaii. They are larger than the atoll and pinnacle zones because they are newer and have not been worn down over so many eras—and also, perhaps, because their volcanoes are more massive. Mauna Loa towers 13,680 feet above the sea, in our day the world's largest active volcano.

Precisely how the raw mountains and valleys of Hawaii turned into a living wilderness is shrouded in mystery. During unknown centuries before men came, somehow the original sea and land birds arrived. Until that time, except for life brought by ocean currents to the coasts, these huge mountaintops were black, lifeless pin points of land in the middle of the Pacific. They were about as far away that land can be from other land. It is some 2,500 miles to the coast of America, 3,800 miles to Japan, and over 2,000 miles to the major Polynesian Islands of the South Pacific.

Yet forest seeds, fern spores, insects, tree snails, and land birds arrived—against the prevailing winds and currents. They are primarily related to Polynesia rather than to

King Kamehameha (above), known as "the Napoleon of the Pacific," unified the Hawaiian Islands in 1810 and ruled them with an iron hand. Two of his subjects are seen below.

In 1820 the first missionaries arrived at Honolulu
(above). They were aghast to find that it had "not
one white cottage, no church spire, not a garden or
a tree to be seen save the grove of coconuts." The
white churchmen were overjoyed, however, to learn
that the pagan idols (below) had been abolished.

139

During Captain Cook's explorations of Hawaii and Alaska in 1778, William Ellis, a surgeon in his crew, pictured the wildlife sighted by the party. He painted these colorful Hawaiian birds as well as the walrus on page 119.

North America. The native Hawaiian forest is a random collection of life somehow brought by storms and birds. It is estimated that if one seed arrived—and its plant succeeded in growing—every 25,000 years since the Hawaiian volcanoes first appeared above the sea, this would be enough to account for the Hawaiian forests. And after that somehow the land was filled with birds, snails, and insects. Of these, almost 95 per cent are peculiar species. They evolved all by themselves, cut off from the other lands of the world.

There are special kinds of sandalwood trees and remarkable hardwoods named koa and ohia, unknown elsewhere. Both plant and animal life evolved in peculiar ways, in part because of the local weather among the volcanoes. On one side of a mountain there is a rain forest, on the other side a desert. One valley is believed to be the wettest place on earth—465 inches of rain per year, over three feet per month. A desert is a mile away.

The nene lives more than a mile up on a volcanic slope where there is almost no water. This goose has no need for webbed feet to swim, so it developed toes for walking. It lives on dry grass and on the berries of little bushes clumped here and there among the lava boulders. Silversword —seen nowhere else in the world— explodes from underneath black lava boulders with leaves like slender knives, dazzling white in the high mountain sunlight. This astonishing variety of trees, birds, and plants was untouched by the evolutionary developments in the rest of the world.

Some five hundred years before the Vikings forged through ice fields, fogs, and storms to catch sight of the northeast coast of America, people in a double canoe first saw the Hawaiian volcanoes above the horizon. They came from Tahiti and Samoa, and this was their last stopping place on a long voyage across the Pacific. It seems incredible that people could travel 2,000 miles over the open ocean in a small sailing canoe. But the Polynesians had been island-hopping and sight-seeing in their canoes for centuries. They were utterly at home in the open seas. They could read the stars, they studied the winds and currents at various seasons, and they knew that sea birds would appear a few hundred miles offshore which they could follow to a landfall.

When later voyagers discovered this volcanic wilderness, its coasts teeming with fish, its luxurious forests filled with brightly colored birds, they sailed southward again across the equator and told their friends about it. After that, many voyages were made back and forth, so that before Columbus discovered the New World these islands were well inhabited.

Before the people came, the untouched wilderness of Hawaii had no furry animals, no snakes, no frogs. The first land mammals to set foot in Hawaii may have been a pair of rats which arrived in the first canoe. The people carried baskets of shells and wooden bowls filled with fruits, seeds, and cuttings of plants. They brought coconut and breadfruit trees—and mosquitoes, fleas, cockroaches, goats, pigs, and dogs.

The volcanic wilderness was now inhabited—but it was still undiscovered and unknown to the civilized world.

In January, 1778, at the height of the American Revolution, an English ship sailing across the Pacific sighted an island. Captain James Cook had been sent by the English government on the age-old project of finding a passage between the Atlantic and Pacific oceans. Explorers had failed to find a waterway through North America from the Atlantic side. So now a ship was sent all the way around Africa, across the Indian Ocean, and across the vast Pacific to see if the elusive passageway might be discovered leading in from the Pacific coast.

This was Captain Cook's third voyage. He had made great discoveries among the South Pacific islands on his first two voyages. Now he found his way to a little island where he and the ship's company spent Christmas day—and so named it Christmas Island. He then set his course northward across the broad Pacific, expecting that his next landfall would be the Aleutian Islands of Alaska.

But some three weeks out of Christmas Island, when they had passed through the usual gales and calms

Cook's once happy relations with the Hawaiians ended abruptly. As the English were about to leave, he was killed by a chief (left foreground). That night the natives roasted Cook's body.

and were close-hauled against the trade winds, a mountainous island appeared in the middle of the Pacific. As Cook drew near, he saw another island to the north. As the first island was then directly into the wind, he steered for the second. Then he saw a third island to the northwest. As they approached, canoes came out and the people in them traded fresh fruits for tools and bits of cloth. Cook was surprised to find that they spoke the same language as the people on Tahiti, 2,000 miles away.

Thus the islands we know as Hawaii were discovered, and the great volcanic wilderness inscribed on the maps of the world. Cook called them the Sandwich Islands, after the Earl of Sandwich, head of Great Britain's Royal Navy. He went on to the coast of Alaska in his fruitless pursuit of the Northwest Passage, but returned to the Hawaiian paradise to spend the winter.

At first Cook was greeted by the natives as a sort of god, but before long the Englishmen and the islanders were in a state of open hostility. In February, 1779, as the ships were preparing to sail away, the natives attacked, and James Cook, the greatest explorer of his time, was stabbed to death.

The coming of the white man to Hawaii wrought changes in the delicate balance of growth and life that was attuned to the rhythms of nature. Thirty-odd years after Captain Cook's expedition, an American sea captain offered to buy all the sandalwood that the subjects of King Kamehameha could cut from the Hawaiian forests. This was a rare wood much treasured by the Chinese for carving and for making incense.

The native nobility of Hawaii amassed enormous treasures of silk and carved luxuries in payment. But by 1825 hardly a sandalwood tree could be found. Agriculture had been neglected in order to cut the trees, and the balance of living of the Hawaiian natives was profoundly upset.

This exploitation of the volcanic wilderness by its discoverers is an example of an over-all pattern that can be traced from Cape Cod to Hawaii. The land seemed so immense and so rich that men grew careless about harvesting its resources. They cut down the forests and diverted the rivers and slaughtered the animals, confident that just over the horizon they would find even greater natural wealth. Finally they began to realize—reluctantly at first, then with growing concern—that their magnificent wilderness heritage was in grave danger.

Farsighted people turned to preservation rather than destruction, to long-range renewal rather than short-term exploitation. It has been a long, hard fight, in many instances begun too late to do any good, and it still continues. Yet Americans seem now to sense the same spirit that moved an Englishman, almost four centuries ago, to write of this land "of huge and unknowen greatnesse. . . ."

*Specimens of a unique type of volcano, the shield
dome, abound in the Hawaiian chain. Unlike the
more familiar cone-shaped volcanoes, Hawaii's are
broad and flat, resulting from relatively tame eruptions of fast-flowing lava. Here some of Peale's
companions study the lower slope of Mauna Loa.*

A geyser of fire and lava belches out of Kilauea Iki (Little Kilauea) in a scene dramatically symbolic of the ever-changing wilderness. After years of fitful slumber, the volcano erupted in a sheet of flame during November, 1959, pouring torrents of molten lava into the surrounding craters and into the dense undergrowth below. At one point the fire fountain soared 1,900 feet into the sky. This photograph is reminiscent of Titian Peale's painting (pages 134–135) done near the same spot more than a century before.

AMERICAN HERITAGE PUBLISHING CO., INC.

PRESIDENT JAMES PARTON

EDITORIAL DIRECTOR JOSEPH J. THORNDIKE, JR.

EDITOR, BOOK DIVISION RICHARD M. KETCHUM

ART DIRECTOR IRWIN GLUSKER

AMERICAN HERITAGE JUNIOR LIBRARY

EDITOR STEPHEN W. SEARS

ART DIRECTOR EMMA LANDAU

ASSISTANT EDITOR DENNIS A. DINAN

CHIEF PICTURE RESEARCHER JULIA B. POTTS

PICTURE RESEARCHER MARY LEVERTY

EDITORIAL ASSISTANT AMY L. RHODES

COPY EDITOR PATRICIA COOPER

ACKNOWLEDGMENTS

The Editors are indebted to the following individuals and institutions for their generous advice and assistance in preparing this book:

The American Museum of Natural History, New York City—George H. Goodwin, Marie E. Macdonald

The American Philosophical Society, Philadelphia—Richard H. Shyrock

The British Museum (Natural History), London—Phyllis T. Edwards, F. C. Sawyer

The British Museum, London—D. F. Snelgrove

Mrs. Jane Horton de Cabanyes, Madrid

Gertrudis Feliu, Jeanne-Françoise Roche, Paris

Mrs. Maureen Green, London

Joseph Hefter, Mexico City

Museo Naval, Madrid—Admiral Julio Guillen, Roberto Barreiro

Princeton University—Dr. Glenn Lowell Jepsen

Mrs. Audrey R. Topping, Moscow

The Yale University Library—Archibald Hanna

FOR FURTHER READING

Augur, Helen. *Passage to Glory*. Doubleday, 1946.

Bakeless, John. *The Eyes of Discovery*. Lippincott, 1950.

Berger, Josef. *Discoverers of the New World*. American Heritage Junior Library, 1960.

Berton, Pierre. *The Klondike Fever*. Knopf, 1958.

Cahalane, Victor H. *Mammals of North America*. Macmillan, 1958.

Carson, Rachel L. *The Edge of the Sea*. Houghton Mifflin, 1955.

Carson, Rachel L. *The Sea Around Us*. Oxford University Press, 1961.

Douglas, William O. *My Wilderness: East to Katahdin*. Doubleday, 1961.

Douglas, William O. *My Wilderness: The Pacific West*. Doubleday, 1960.

Farb, Peter. *Face of North America*. Harper & Row, 1963.

Krutch, Joseph Wood. *The Desert Year*. Sloane, 1952.

Krutch, Joseph Wood. *Grand Canyon*. Sloane, 1958.

Life Nature Library: *The Desert,* 1961; *The Forest,* 1961; *The Mountains,* 1962. Time, Inc.

Matthiessen, Peter. *Wildlife in America*. Viking, 1959.

Peattie, Roderick, editor. *The Pacific Coast Ranges*. Vanguard, 1946.

Sanderson, Ivan T. *The Continent We Live On*. Random House, 1961.

Stegner, Wallace. *Beyond the Hundredth Meridian*. Houghton Mifflin, 1954.

Teale, Edwin Way. *Adventures in Nature*. Dodd, Mead, 1959.

Teale, Edwin Way. *Autumn Across America*. Dodd, Mead, 1956.

Thoreau, Henry David. *Walden*. Edwin Way Teale, editor. (Great Illustrated Classics), Dodd, Mead, 1955.

Tilden, Freeman. *The National Parks*. Knopf, 1951.

A California cowboy, sketched by Titian Peale, gallops recklessly after a flock of wild geese.

Index

Bold face indicates pages on which illustrations appear